Carousel Horse
Carving

An Instructional Workbook
in 1/3 Scale

By
KEN HUGHES

Box 7948
Lancaster, PA 17604

Thanks to Thelma White for her much appreciated review of this material. Thanks also to Sherilyn Tharp for her input, and to Tony White for his contribution of the two clamping device ideas. Last but not least, thanks to Ben Shaw for sharing his shop and for his ongoing support regarding this project.

Copyright © 1996 Fox Chapel Publishing Company Inc.
Revised Third Edition of Carousel Horse Carving: An Instruction Workbook originally published in 1987 by Heritage Arts Press.
Publisher: Alan Giagnocavo
Project Editor: Ayleen Stellhorn
ISBN# 1-56523-072-8

To order your copy of this book,
please send check or money order
for $24.95 plus $2.50 shipping to:
Fox Books Orders
Box 7948
Lancaster PA 17604-7948

♞ TABLE OF CONTENTS ♞

♞ *INTRODUCTION* ♞

The design of the carousel horse you'll be carving was inspired by a Charles Carmel "stander" circa 1915. A stander is a carousel horse in a standing pose with the hooves of three legs touching the floor while the fourth leg (either of the front legs) is raised up. Some carousels have standers with four-on-the-floor, but most have three. And, in case you're curious about other carousel poses, a horse suspended on a pole with all four legs raised off the floor is called a "jumper," while a horse with only the front legs raised up is called a "prancer."

A few characteristics have been modified on this scaled down design of an early 20th century carousel horse, but the symmetry and overall bearing have been retained. Before you get started, here are a few thoughts pertaining to the project.

Carousel horses are garish, magical creatures that tantalize the imagination and reinforce the notion that there is still some of the child present in all of us. These enchanting animals are made of wood, glass eyes and artificial jewels and are, by and large, exaggerations of real horses. Unlike carousel horses, real horses are composed of flesh, bones, hair and bodily fluids. If you keep these obvious distinctions in mind as you embark on this creative journey it will mercifully save you from trying to turn out a down-to-the-last-eyelash reproduction of a real horse. This type of approach to carving a horse usually includes the use of calipers and other precision-like instruments. What's the reason for bringing this up? Because if you're carving a horse for the first time, approaching the project in this fussy, overly exacting way can transform the creative process into something resembling a calculating science. And this, in turn, will interfere with what should be largely an aesthetic, interpretive experience rather than an attempt to achieve absolute perfection.

The instructions in this book are presented as a series of guidelines. There are no unwavering formulas for carving a carousel horse, whether it's a standard size or a reduced size such as the one you'll be working on. Although your best bet is to follow the guidelines to some degree, don't hesitate to give yourself some free rein. If you find that you're occasionally moving around in the order of things or maybe getting a little ahead, it's not likely this will result in your fouling anything up. However, it's a good idea to stick to the guidelines in those instances where it's obvious that you should not move forward too early.

FIGURE 1 — *Before you begin to plan your carving, review reference material about horses, including photographs, videotapes, live animals and even toy horses. An anatomy chart of a horse is shown on page iv.*

If you keep a positive attitude and don't hurry, you'll almost certainly turn out a first-class carving job. To further ensure this prediction, it's suggested that you study photographs and illustrations of horses, any horses at first, just to get acquainted with the general anatomy. *(See Figure 1.)* Take several rolls of film to a carousel, if there's one in your area. Isolate details in your photographs: face, mane, neck, chest, legs and so on. Study the photographs in the "Photo Gallery." Several good photographic books about carousel animals are available for purchase and can serve as valuable visual aids as you carve.

The old adage "it takes time to create quality" wasn't dreamed up by some advertising agency with a large brewery account. It's been around for quite awhile. You might consider writing it down and hanging it at eye level over your work space. A rush job usually looks like a rush job, so don't hurry things. By working at an even, non-frantic pace, you'll no doubt avoid making unwanted mistakes, plus it will help you maintain an admirable safety record.

As mentioned above, the main purpose of this book is to instruct and guide you as you carve. Therefore, information about the history of the carousel and data about the carvers has not been included here. There are a few good books in print that deal with both these subjects in detail.

In a few instances, you'll notice information addressed to beginning carvers. These occasional references are for individuals who've had very little, if any, exposure to carving. If you've never carved anything before, or even had a few sessions in a beginning woodcarving class, you're a truly brave individual. Although making a small carousel horse does not

---

🎠 **Carousel Horse Carving** 🎠

call for a high level of sophistication in wood carving, some basic hands-on experience will give you a foundation of knowledge and prepare you for dealing with minor problems that could possibly occur.

On the other hand, from time to time, someone comes along with a so-called in-born talent, like the natural musician who can pick up an instrument, feel his or her way along, and create somewhat imperfect but somehow beautiful music. If you feel self-assured enough to go forward in carving a horse with no prior carving experience, good luck to you. It should prove to be an interesting challenge. If you do not feel so self-assured, consider taking a basic woodcarving course before starting on the horse. The boost of confidence you'll gain will be worth the time and effort.

It will be to your advantage to read through the entire material, briefly at least, before beginning work on the horse. A light once-over will give you a general idea of what to expect. Then, as you finally get underway, you can take your time carefully reading over the text and looking over the photographs that relate to the area you're working on.

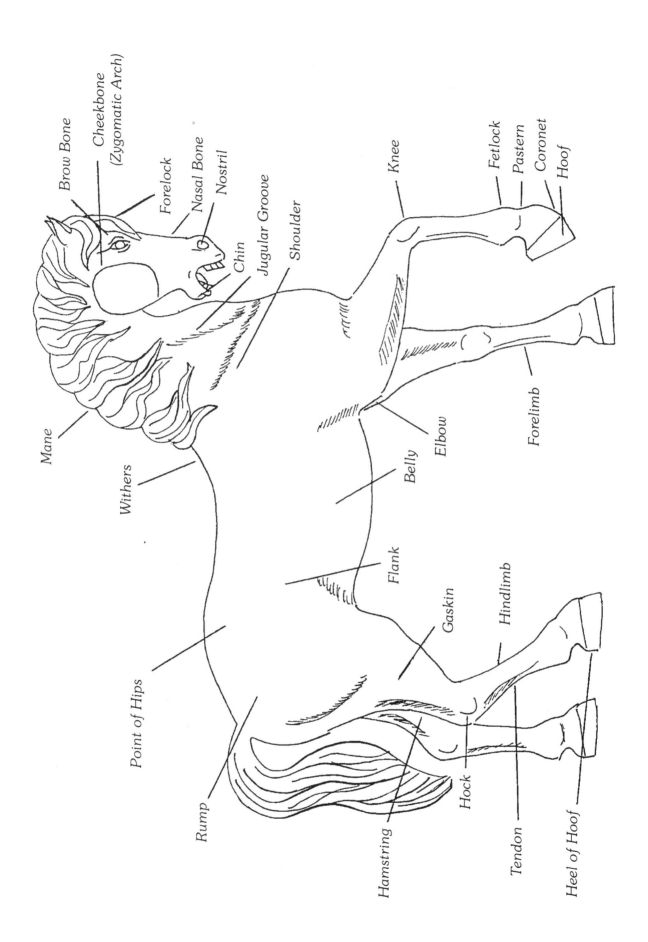

☙ *CHAPTER I* ☙

MATERIAL

The wood of first choice for carving a carousel horse is basswood, which is referred to as a soft hardwood by the lumber industry. Carousel horse carvers have traditionally used basswood, poplar, pine, cottonwood, alder, mahogany and other varieties of carving wood. Sometimes a particular type of wood is preferred by one carver and rejected by another. The reasons for choosing one type of wood over another are sometimes practical, sometimes arbitrary. If basswood is unavailable in your area or scarce in the quantity or dimensions required, look for poplar or a good quality sugar pine.

Basswood is given first preference for two main reasons. First, it's an exceptionally good carving wood, particularly for detail work. The other reason is the end grain. There's not a whole lot to be done on the end grain when carving a carousel horse, but what there is can potentially become a miserable and frustrating experience. End grain is never much fun to carve, but with basswood it's much easier to handle than it is on some other woods (for instance, poor quality pine) because the fiber is more firm. Also, it's unusual to find knots in basswood sold at commercial lumber yards, which is a big plus. Although a few knots do occasionally appear on a board, they can most likely be "buried" on the inside of a laminated section.

One drawback with basswood comes during the final stages of sanding. The surface of the wood tends to maintain a slight fuzziness even when a finer grit sandpaper is used. Applying a coat of sanding sealer to the entire surface of the wood will cause the fuzziness to settle down during the final lap to the finish.

As far as length goes, when you purchase the lumber watch out for boards that are twisted or otherwise severely warped. A slight bow is not uncommon in a long board, especially if it's been stacked with other boards and left out in the elements for several months. A serious warp, on the other hand, should definitely be avoided. Check to see if the boards are straight by sighting them lengthwise. Do your best to get straight-as-an-arrow boards with a minimum of defects at the ends and along the edges where minor problems occasionally turn up. Don't get chintzy

---

about going a few feet over when you select the lumber, in case by happenstance you find yourself needing additional wood.

TOOLS

Every carousel horse, as it's carved, evolves with unique qualities that the carver attributes to it. Some people like intricate carvings such as eagles, cherubs, scarves, flowers and baroque-style piping around the saddle, blanket and trappings. Others prefer finely carved muscles and a full complement of body and head straps emblazoned with jewels and other glitz. And still others go for a subdued, functional look. It's the style you decide on that will dictate both the type and number of tools you'll need after the rough-shaping is out of the way. Obviously, a more basic style will require fewer tools than one that is exotic and elaborate with numerous details.

Four tool lists are included in this chapter. The first tool list outlines the tools needed to construct the horse blank. The second list represents those tools that will be most helpful for roughing out the basic shape. The final two lists deal with tools and materials that can be useful as you make further progress on the horse. Please be aware that the tools on the lists are suggestions, not gospel. Any number of variations will work. Feel your way along to determine what you'll need as the horse begins to gain more focus. When you see this sign (+) on a list, it indicates that a certain tool will be helpful during the onset of the fine-shaping stage. Buying quality tools can get expensive, so be sure you don't accumulate too many too early. Tool references throughout the text are mostly presented in general terms, such as "medium shallow gouge" or "large deep gouge." In some cases, more specific references are made.

Keep a variety of tools nearby and choose the one you'll need for the cut, trim, score line or whatever has to be done at the time. There is no predetermined number of tools to use. The best place to purchase tools is at a woodcarving supply store or a woodcarving supply outlet. Another possible source for woodcarving tools is a flea market. Other sources are newspaper classifieds, second-hand tool shops, art supply stores and, in some cases, hardware or handyman stores.

TOOL LIST FOR CONSTRUCTING THE HORSE BLANK

The shop equipment that will help you the most in the construction of the horse blank is as follows. If you don't have access to all of the larger equipment listed here, don't let that discourage you from going ahead. If you combine ingenuity with common sense, you'll be able to come up with several smaller power tools and hand tools that will help you to construct a horse blank ready for carving. But you better keep an extra supply of elbow grease nearby.

(+) BANDSAW

You'll need a bandsaw to saw out the many contours on the various parts of the horse after you've laminated and joined the wood. Of all the power equipment listed, this one is the most essential.

TABLE SAW

If you have a table saw it can be used to make crosscuts and rip cuts on the laminated boards. A table saw will make particularly smooth, even surfaces along the edges of the two outer sections on the body, an important step in the construction of the horse. However, if you don't have access to a table saw a bandsaw can be substituted, or even a radial arm saw.

PLANER

Use a thickness planer (also referred to as mill and plane) to surface the boards to your specifications. This may not be necessary if they've already been surfaced at a lumber yard. A portable electric planer can be used for trimming edges and planing smaller surfaces.

JOINTER

Unless you're experienced at using a hand-held plane, a jointer can be a godsend for trimming along the edges of the boards during the process of lamination. *Do not* try end grain on a jointer.

BELT/DISC FLOOR-MODEL SANDER

This one-two combination will give you consistently smooth surfaces on the flat areas of the three sets of leg parts that have to be made into whole legs. A belt/disc sander can also be used on the bottom surface of the head and the top and bottom surfaces of the neck, which ultimately will be glued to other smooth surfaces. A portable electric sander can be used as long as the belt is wide enough, but don't expect the results to be as consistently even as you'd get with a standard belt/disc sander.

(+) CLAMPS

Initially, you'll have to glue some of the boards together before you saw out the various parts. Handscrews or carpenter's clamps are excellent clamps for this task. Try to use handscrews that will open to at least a 10" capacity so you'll have enough room to maneuver the wood jaws to gain a secure grip on the wood. Consider borrowing an armful of handscrews for a few days if you know someone who has some; they are not cheap. Maybe you could rent some from a woodshop nearby.

I-beam clamps are also good for laminating the boards in the very early stages, but they are not as versatile as handscrews. They are also harder to come by.

When you get ready to glue the neck to the body you'll need two bar (sometimes called "pipe") clamps. Additionally, a band belt, which has an adjustable cam-like apparatus, can be looped over the neck and body as an auxiliary clamp while the glue sets up.

MISCELLANEOUS TOOLS AND SUPPLIES FOR CONSTRUCTING THE HORSE BLANK

The following list of miscellaneous tools and supplies is what you'll need to complete the horse blank. In a few instances, you can improvise. One example is in the case of the spring miter clamps.

(+) SCREWDRIVER
Use any medium size screw driver as long as the blade will fit into a 1/2" diameter hole.

SPRING MITER CLAMPS
If you're not familiar with these little items, there's a photograph showing them in action further on in the text *(See Figure 17A)*. They are used to keep tension on the leg parts as you glue the three pairs together. A tool called a "spreader" is used to apply these clamps. Four spring clamps should be enough. You could improvise by using springs cut from old chairs or sofas.

(+) ELECTRIC HAND DRILL
A 3/8" variable speed portable drill is sufficient for drilling the holes for dowels and screws. The drill will be used throughout different stages of construction.

(+) DRILL BITS
You'll need a few spade bits (wood boring bits) found in standard packaged sets, foremost of these being a 1/2" diameter bit. You will also need a 1 1/8" diameter bit for making ear holes, unless you choose to make the ears from a smaller diameter dowel. In addition, you'll need a few twist bits for drilling smaller diameter holes, more specifically a 13/64" bit and a 1/8" bit. Finally, you'll need a second 1/8" twist bit that is six inches in length. This extra long bit will be used for drilling a hole through the head and into the neck.

(+) HAND PLANE
If you don't have access to a jointer, a jack plane or smoothing plane can be used for trimming the edges of the boards and, later, wider surfaces after the boards have been laminated.

(+) DOWEL PEGS
A length of 1/2" diameter dowel can serve as a source for dowel pegs. These dowel pieces are used as part of the binding process in gluing the parts together. The length will vary as needed. Fluted dowel pins (pegs) can be purchased at some hardware stores.

(+) SCREWS
You'll need two 2" #10 roundhead screws and two 2½" #10's. You'll also need a 3" #10 screw as well as a package of washers to go with all of the screws. If you can't find roundhead screws in these lengths, flathead screws will have to do.

(+) GLUE
Yellow glue is a reliable glue for laminating the boards and for gluing the various parts together. White glue is okay, but yellow glue is better. *No epoxy.*

(+) PENCIL
A dark-leaded pencil will come in handy throughout the project.

METAL DOWEL CENTERS
These spike-tipped marking implements come in sets of six. They are inexpensive and a great help in accurately marking the spot where a matching hole should be drilled as you join the upper and lower leg parts, neck to body, head to neck, and tail to rump.

AWL
This punch tool is used to make starter holes for the drill bits.

RULER
Use a long ruler or yard stick as a marking aid for drawing straight lines needed for several cuts along the length of the wood.

PAPER TOWELS
Keep a roll of paper towels nearby to wipe off excess glue as you laminate the boards and join the leg sections.

TOOL LIST FOR
BASIC SHAPING AND CARVING

MALLET
Any good woodcarving mallet, as long as it isn't too small. Make sure you get one that will do the job when you'll be using either medium or large woodcarving tools.

LARGE DEEP GOUGE
A #7 (30mm) is a good size to use, but almost any large deep gouge will do as long as you keep it sharp. Good for chunking out excess wood in the early stages of the rough carving.

LARGE SHALLOW GOUGE
A #5 (30mm) or a #3 (30mm). Good for shaping and removing wood in the rough-shaping stage on the body and neck.

DRAW KNIFE

Try to get one with a long sloping bevel on the cutting edge, rather than a short steep bevel. Good for basic shaping all over the body. Especially handy for quick removal of wood in the early stage of the carving. If you decide to use this tool get one with a straight, not curved blade

SPOKESHAVE

This tool is a pleasure to work with. It's sort of a combination mini-draw knife and hand plane. Handy when shaping the legs and cleaning up the rounded surfaces on the body. A medium size is best for working on the horse.

RASP

Any medium size rasp with a handle. Used to clean up the surface of the wood to see where you're at and to shape the basic contours on the body and legs. Don't get one that is too coarse or overly fine, just somewhere in between.

SAW RASP

Another tool that helps in shaping and filing off rough surfaces is a saw rasp. This is an amazing two-sided filing tool with numerous criss-crossed surrogated edges. One filing surface is medium coarse, the other side fine. A long, tubular version is also available and can be used to shape curves and rounded areas.

HANDSCREW

This is a clamp with rugged, hardwood jaws. For a more detailed description, see "Clamping The Wood," in this chapter.

TOOL LIST FOR
FINER SHAPING AND CARVING

(+) MEDIUM SHALLOW GOUGE

Either a #5 (20mm) or #6 (25mm). Useful at various times for finer carving on the body, legs and head.

SMALL SHALLOW GOUGE

Either a #5 (5mm) or #3 (5mm). Used for close-up work as you get more involved in details. A very good size to work with.

MEDIUM CHISEL

A #1 (20mm) straight chisel, useful for making stop cuts and for removing excess wood around the trappings and blanket.

(+) MEDIUM V-PARTING TOOL

A medium angle 8mm tool, useful for scoring the saddle, trappings and mane. Different companies use different numbering systems for parting tools.

SMALL V-PARTING TOOL
Either a medium angle 3mm or a 4mm. For carving around the trappings and on any small detail work, depending on how much detail you're planning to put on the horse.

MEDIUM DEEP VEINER
This tool can be used for carving on the face and for scooping out wood between the segments of the mane. Try either #11 (10mm) or #9 (7mm). Not an absolute must, but if you have one it'll come in handy.

(+) CHIP CARVING KNIFE
Also known as a bench knife, this tool is indispensable for carving the ears and for carving around the eyelids. Also, it's good for making stop cuts when necessary. If you get pretty good with a chip carving knife it can do the work of several tools, such as a v-parting tool and, in some instances, a skew. There are many variations of chip carving knives, but the best type for this project is shown in *Figure 2*. If you only use a

FIGURE 2 — *A chip carving knife, or bench knife, is the ideal tool for carving details on a carousel horse. Among other things, it is used specifically for carving ears and eyelids.*

handful of tools to carve the horse, make sure a chip carving knife is among them. It's an important detail carving tool.

SKEW
This is a chisel-like tool with the cutting edge on an angle that can vary on

different types of skews from about 15° to 45°. Very effective as a hand-held tool to shave off wood around the trappings and blanket. A #1 (12mm) is a good compromise size to use for this kind of trimming. This is another tool that is not really necessary in order to complete the carving of the horse. If you own a skew, use it. If not, don't bother spending money on one.

RIFFLERS

Be sure to keep at least one small riffler around, two if possible. The riffler should have curved heads at each end, or at least a curved head at one end. These little filing tools are excellent for shaping, refining and cleaning up detail work. Additionally, they're a big help when you're working on the strands of the mane and tail.

(+) HALF-ROUND RASP

A medium-sized metal rasp will do the job. A rasp can be used on pasterns (at the lower part of each leg) and for miscellaneous shaping of rounded areas on the body. If you don't currently own a rasp but plan on purchasing one, get one with a medium scraping surface. And make sure it has a handle.

Note: *As a substitute for, or in addition to, a rasp or surform you can use sandpaper rolled up or wrapped around a dowel.*

MISCELLANEOUS TOOLS AND MATERIALS

SHARPENING STONES

Try to get a combination India bench stone, coarse on one side and fine on the other. Also, get a slip stone for removing burrs from the other side of the cutting edge. Wet/dry sandpaper, about #320 grit, can be used in a pinch.

YELLOW OR WHITE GLUE

Most brands found at hardware stores are good. Yellow glues set up fast and make a strong bond. They're a little rougher on sharp cutting edges than white glue, but not enough to make a fuss about.

PENCIL

Buy a thick, dark-leaded pencil for drawing designs onto the wood and for marking guidelines throughout the carving.

SANDPAPER

Five or six sheets of #60 grit and about a dozen sheets of #80 and #120 grit. Assuming you plan on painting the horse, you won't need to go beyond #120 grit.

COPING SAW

This saw is used for cutting out the back of the top section of the teeth on the head piece. What does this mean? Don't be too anxious to find out about the head. It's a real workout.

WOOD FILLER
If you accidentally take off more then you intended to here and there, a good filler can be a godsend. Store-bought commercial wood fillers are not that reliable for many of the larger spaces you might want to fill or areas you might want to build up. For minor surface problems they're okay, but don't rely on them beyond that.

There are some filler products manufactured primarily for industry use, for example for the repair and restoration of wooden boats. Wood epoxy dries hard, but can be carved, filed, sanded and painted. Pint size jars are the most suitable amounts to use for this project. If you can find wood epoxy, by all means use it if you want to build up some area or otherwise alter something on the horse.

SPACKLING PASTE
This is a pre-mixed patching compound. It can be used as a surface filler during the final stages of completion, but prior to applying any sanding sealer or undercoating to the wood. Spackle is good for filling in small, shallow holes, pitted areas and rough, hard-to-work surfaces such as end grain after you've gone about as far as you can with sandpaper. Especially handy for filling and smoothing the nostril holes. *(See Figure 3.)*

FIGURE 3 — *Wood epoxy is especially useful for filling in unwanted cuts and building up certain areas of the horse. It dries hard and can be carved, filed, sanded and painted.*

HAND-HELD SAW
A crosscut saw of standard size, or any basic household saw. It will be

used to saw out a division in the rump area. A smaller saw is actually easier to maneuver in this area, but don't bother going out and spending money on one if you have a garden variety relic around the house or can borrow one for a one-shot procedure.

VARIABLE SPEED ELECTRIC HAND DRILL
You'll need a portable hand drill for several reasons that you'll discover as you get further along with the horse.

SHARP TOOLS

Be sure you keep a sharp cutting edge on all your carving tools, including the draw knife if you plan on using one. It makes a significant difference in the progress you make and the quality of the results. Tools with dull edges will hold you back. And they can possibly be the cause of a nasty injury along the way because you'll have to expend so much physical effort to make any headway. You'll see how this could occur when you get into the carving. Another negative about dull-edged tools is that after working with them for a while it can have an adverse effect on your attitude toward the carving. If the effort to make the tools do their job becomes too great, over a period of time it could result in your becoming discouraged and losing interest in following through to completion.

A discourse on how to sharpen tools is not forthcoming. If you do not know how to sharpen tools, purchase a basic woodcarving book that describes how or try to contact someone who will show you how on a one-to-one basis. Another possibility is to go around to a woodcarving shop or to an ongoing shop class for some instruction. A personal demonstration on sharpening is worth a thousand photographs and written words.

HELPFUL TIPS
FOR BEGINNING CARVERS

You don't always need to use a mallet in conjunction with a carving tool. In the initial stages of rough carving, yes, you will most definitely need to use one when you're working with large gouges. Later, however, when you need more control removing wood in a particular area or for carving details, try guiding the tools with both hands. Apply as much pressure as the particular circumstances call for. One hand should grip the handle and push, while the other hand holds the steel below the handle and guides the business end of the tool. When you hold any tools that have sharp cutting edges, *always make sure both hands are behind the cutting edge. (See Figure 4.)* Never grip or steady the wood with one hand out in front of the tool's cutting edge. If you're inexperienced in using carving tools with both hands, find a few pieces of scrap wood to practice on. Secure the wood with a clamp or vise.

FIGURE 4 — *Safety should always be first and foremost in your mind while you are carving. Keep your tools sharp and be sure both hands are behind the cutting edge of the tool you are using.*

As you're working on the horse try to carve in the general direction of the grain whenever possible. (There'll be many instances, of course, when you can't do that.) Often, you'll be carving at a slight angle to the grain, which is fine. In fact, there's nothing unusual about carving at a bit of an angle to the grain, as long as you travel in the general direction of the grain. Avoid carving directly across the grain if your tools are dull. The sharper the cutting edges of your tools, the smoother the going will be if there are circumstances where you have to carve across the grain.

CLAMPING THE WOOD

Securing the body and the individual legs as you carve them can become a major annoyance until you get the hang of it, by which time you're almost finished. The three most practical devices for holding the various sections are as follows: a wooden hand clamp (or handscrew as they're called) that opens to a 10" capacity, a bench vise (jaw vise) with an 8" to 10" capacity and an adjustable band belt or strap. This is not to say that you'll need all three of these clamping devices, but you should definitely have a wooden hand clamp or two. They're used for securing the body on its side, as well as the individual legs in an endless number of positions. *(See Figures 5-1, 5-2.)*

Band belts are useful for working on the body, also. These belts often come in bright colors and include a tiny wrench which is used for tightening a ratchet gizmo to secure the work. *(See Figure 6.)* Some band belts have a self-contained ratchet apparatus.

FIGURES 5-1 AND 5-2 — *Placing your carving in a vise or clamp will hold the wood steady and free both of your hands. Hand clamps or a bench vise are two good choices.*

A metal vise, or jaw vise as they are often referred to, is more limited for working on the body since there isn't enough room to maneuver around once the wood is clamped in the jaws. If you have a vise that is attached to a workbench and plan to use it to some degree, be sure to place a scrap of wood on the inside of each metal jaw plate. Wood scraps will help to avoid making deep indentations in the side of the horse, most important as you make further progress.

Another method of clamping the body is with a couple of metal bar or

FIGURE 6 — *An adjustable belt or strap is another good choice for holding your carving securely in place while you work. Old tire tubes of different lengths can often be used in lieu of a belt or strap.*

pipe clamps. The problem here is that it can quickly become a royal pain in the afterdeck, because you have to insert scraps of wood between the horse's body and the jaws of the clamps. And be sure of this, you'll be frequently clamping, unclamping and re-clamping these or any other portable clamping devices you use. Since you'll be using these metal clamps in the same way you'd be using wooden hand clamps (handscrews), that is for quick release and frequent re-clamping, go with the wooden clamps. They're more versatile, especially for securing the legs.

MORE ABOUT CLAMPING

In addition to the methods already described for holding the body, there's another alternative to consider. It's an easily constructed portable platform that can be secured in a bench vise. The body of the horse is placed on its side on the platform, after which a band belt is looped around both the body and the platform. *(See Figure 6.)* The ratchet apparatus on the belt is then turned as tightly as possible. The result is a surprisingly secure, temporary union of the body and the platform.

To make one of these platforms, saw off a 30" long piece of wood from a 2" x 4" board, hereafter referred to as a two-by-four. Next, saw off a 30" long piece from a 1" x 8" length of pine shelving or any piece of scrapwood the equivalent size. Hammer about five or six finishing nails part way into the center line of this board, which will soon be a platform. The nails should be distributed along the length of the board. Next, place the two-by-four on its edge. Balance the 1" x 8" board flat on the edge of

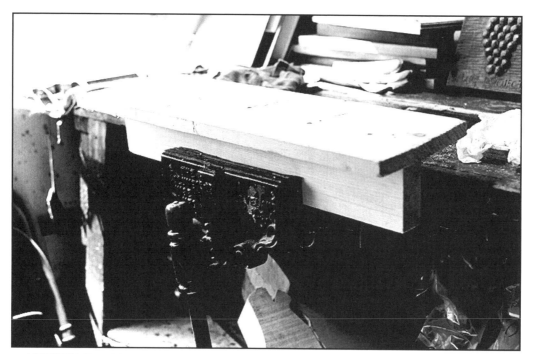

FIGURE 7 — This clamping device, made from a two-by-four clamped to a bench vise and two yoke-like cradles (shown in Figure 8), is especially useful when working on the legs.

the two-by-four and hammer the nails the rest of the way into the two-by-four. You now have a portable work platform, limited though it may be. *(See Figure 7.)*

There's another clamping device that can be helpful as you're carving

FIGURE 8 — The yoke-like cradles fit into holes drilled into the two-by-four. Drilling a number of holes in the two-by-four will allow you to adjust the position of the cradles for larger or smaller legs.

the legs. *(See Figure 8.)* It works like this. A three-foot length from a two-by-four is clamped in a bench vise. The two-by-four has about six ½" diameter holes drilled through the edge. Two wooden yolk or cradle-like holders (each with a ½" diameter dowel peg glued into the bottom) are placed in any two holes in the two-by-four that are close to each other. Then, place one of the legs so that it's resting on these two cradles at whatever angle seems to work. Next, a band belt is looped around the board and over the middle part of the leg. The cradles will pivot slightly as the belt is tightened. When it's secured, the leg can be worked on and more than likely it will not budge an inch.

To construct this device, drill six ½" diameter holes through the edge of a three foot long two-by-four. Drill the holes about two inches apart. Next, the wooden cradles are made by cutting out two blocks of wood about 4½" x 3½" from a two-by-four, or any comparable scrap wood. Also, cut out a couple of 2¾" x 2½" blocks, in case you want to try some smaller cradles. Saw out a V-shape from each of the blocks, making the bottom of the V-shape end at about the half-way point. Now drill a ½" diameter hole approximately 1" deep into the bottom of each block. Put the blocks aside for now. The pegs that fit into the bottom of the blocks are made by sawing off four 3" lengths from a ½" diameter dowel. Glue the pegs into the holes in the blocks. That should do it. You can work on one leg at a time, or two if you have another band belt. *(See Figure 9.)*

CARVING PROGRESSION

A carousel horse is carved most efficiently in separate parts rather than as

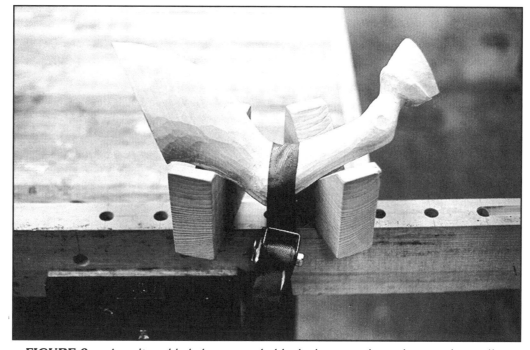

FIGURE 9 — *An adjustable belt or strap holds the leg securely in place on the cradles.*

a single unit. Each part is usually worked on individually with the carver shuttling back and forth from one part to the next, then back again. The reason for all this shuttling is to keep the carving in balance as it progresses. It will keep you from getting carried away on one part of the horse. In other words, it's not a good idea to reduce a leg down to a finely carved specimen ready for sanding, then move on to the next leg and the next after that. No matter how well things seem to be going, try to restrain yourself from going all the way. A little old-fashioned virtue never hurt anyone.

Do not glue the legs, head or tail to the body until you're in the *final stages of sanding your carousel horse*. By that time you will have temporarily assembled the horse a few times in order to blend the various parts together. This blending is initially begun by making marks on the wood, after which the horse is disassembled and the carving refinements are continued.

Eventually, you'll reach a point where you've carved all that you can carve, or want to carve, and will have started to sand the surface smooth. This will be the time to consider gluing the parts together into a whole. Gluing will be mentioned again later in the text.

IF SOMETHING BREAKS

In the unfortunate event that one of the legs, or the head or the tail, gets somehow fouled up, don't get discouraged. It's a problem that is extraordinarily unexceptional. What you can do is simply replace the damaged part. This refers, of course, to major damage such as: too much carved off; severe break in a limb; deep accidental gouge cut leaving the strength of the damaged area in doubt and so on. The way to fix this type of problem is to purchase additional basswood, trace around the outline of the problem part, saw it out and begin carving again. If you're unable to find basswood, then sugar pine or another soft carving wood will have to do. It's not an ideal way to join the wood, as a whole, but it *will* work.

In order to get the right thickness, buy as many pieces of wood as it takes to collectively make up the thickness you need. Naturally, if you're able to locate thick enough chunks of carving wood to do the job, this lamination business will not apply to you. When you have enough pieces of wood to form the desired thickness, glue the boards flat against each other. (If you're not familiar with this gluing procedure, it's what is known as "lamination.") Be sure to spread glue over each surface to be glued.

When the boards are all in place, clamp them securely at several points on all sides. Wipe off any excess glue that squeezes out. When the glue has dried thoroughly, place the part you're duplicating onto the laminated piece of wood and draw around the outline. Then, it's merely a matter of sawing out the part you need and planing or sanding the surface, or surfaces, to be joined.

If part of a leg breaks off, and it's a jagged but clean break, glue the

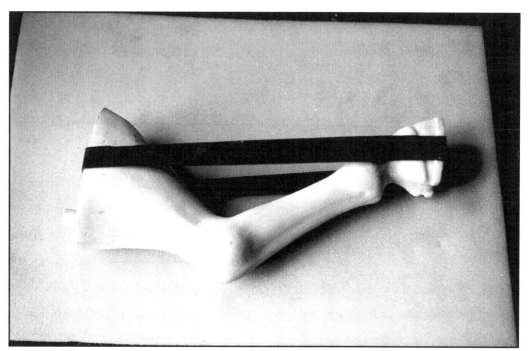

FIGURE 10 — *Jagged but clean breaks are easily fixed. Old tire tubes are ideal for holding the broken pieces of a leg in place while the glue dries.*

two pieces together with either yellow or white glue, but *not epoxy glue*. Epoxy is too hard on the cutting edges of your tools. Use whatever means you have at hand to secure the pieces together while the glue is setting. Spring miter clamps make excellent miniclamps to use if a break has occurred at a joint. You'll need a special tool for spreading open the springs. Not surprisingly, this tool is called a spreader. Additionally, old tire tubes tied together into short, tight bands also make reliable clamps for applying pressure when gluing up legs. *(See Figure 10.)*

For a stronger bond, use the following procedure. Drill a $\frac{1}{2}$" diameter hole into the joint where the two pieces fit together. Next, saw off a $\frac{3}{4}$" long peg from a $\frac{1}{2}$" diameter dowel. Then, rub glue on the dowel peg and squeeze a few drops into the hole you drilled. Insert the peg into the hole, giving it a gentle, but firm tap to make sure it's in all the way. Chisel, file or saw off any nub that protrudes above the surface. Continue where you left off.

DEFINITIONS OF COMMON WOODCARVING TERMS

The following definitions represent a few terms used in the workbook with which you should become familiar:

SCORE LINE
A score line, or scoring mark, refers to a shallow cut made in the wood. It's an establishing cut that precedes additional carving. Often a score line is used as a guide for a stop cut.

FIGURE 11 — *A carousel horse starts with many blanks assembled into one horse. Before you begin to carve, temporarily assemble the blank and make any adjustments that are needed to ensure the horse will stand on its own.*

STOP CUT

A stop cut is a cut made into the wood that establishes a depth limit. Excess wood is then carved or shaved away up to the stop cut, most often from a right angle. The stop cut prevents the cutting edge of a tool from going beyond a specific point. This procedure can be repeated over and over until the desired depth is reached on whatever part of the horse you're carving on at the time.

RELIEF

When something is carved in "relief," it means that a portion of wood is left protruding out from the surrounding wood. When you make stop cuts around the saddle, for instance, and remove the wood outside it, the saddle will then stand out in relief. The blanket, head straps and body straps will all be carved in relief.

TEMPLATE

A template is a pattern that is cut out of paper, cardboard or other material. The pattern can be a simple shape or an intricate design. When the pattern is cut out, it is held against the surface of whatever it is that is being worked on. Then, the outline of the pattern is traced over with a pencil or other marking implement.

Before you begin carving, assemble the parts of the horse into a single unit. *(See Figure 11.)* When you're satisfied that everything fits together as it should and that the horse stands fairly level, unscrew the parts, disassemble the horse and grab some tools.

♞ *CHAPTER II* ♞

GENERAL

The first order of business is the construction of a wood blank for a small carousel horse. The horse blank described in the following pages is constructed of solid wood, as opposed to the so-called "coffin-style" construction. Coffin-style is the type of hollow body, and often hollow neck, construction used on most of the standard-sized carousel animals carved almost three generations ago during the heyday of the carousel. These larger bodies were made hollow for several practical reasons: the usual economic considerations (using less material); weight reduction for transporting many wooden animals when necessary; and avoiding the negative effects of weather changes on the wood for those carousels exposed to the elements.

For the most part, the above stated reasons for hollow construction do not apply to a scaled-down horse 27" high and 29" long, which is the approximate size of the carousel horse you'll end up with if you make one based on the pattern design.

WOOD DIMENSIONS

The total amount of wood required for all the parts except the neck, which is described in detail below, is 1" x 8½" x 28'. The breakdown is as follows:

BODY (1" x 8½" x 16')
The body of the horse is made up of three separate sections that are laminated into one unit. There's a right body section, a left body section and a middle section. Each of the two *outer* body sections should be approximately 2⅝" thick, give or take ⅛". Each outer section is made up of three boards, usually.

The *middle* section of the body should be about 2" thick or slightly less. This section is made up of two boards glued together. If you get rough-surfaced lumber, which will be closer to 1" net thickness than will milled lumber, you'll have the right thickness.

HEAD, LEGS AND TAIL (1" x 8½" x 12')
The 12' length is a slightly liberal estimate by a few feet. The head, legs

and tail (as well as the ears, which can be made up from scraps of wood) can be sawed out of boards of the same width as that used for the body. Or not. In other words, you can use lumber that is 8½" wide or an odd width, as long as the templates for these small parts will fit onto the wood.

The leg parts are made from three boards glued together so that the thickness of the legs corresponds to the approximate thickness of the two outer body sections.

NECK (1" x 10" x 5')
The reason for the 10" width is because on this design the mane should, ideally, angle diagonally downward toward the front of the horse. The carving will be much easier with the grain going in the same direction as the flow of the mane.

If you just can't find a wide enough board, use whatever board width is available upon which the neck template will fit with the grain of the wood going in a horizontal direction from the front of the neck to the back. When you get ready to carve, draw the segments of the mane onto the neck at a more horizontal angle than you would have if you were using a 10" wide board.

Note: *Stay fairly close to the thicknesses recommended to keep the overall proportions relative to the height of the horse.*

COMMENTS ABOUT THE WOOD

If you plan to purchase your wood at a lumber yard be aware that any lumber that has been milled is usually not the thickness specified. For example, when a 1" thick board is milled on both sides at a lumber yard, it's really around $^{13}/_{16}$" thick. Sometimes only ¾". As previously mentioned, try to use the thicknesses suggested as guidelines, but do not become concerned about *minor* differences in thickness. If you're able to use a planer yourself, buy the lumber rough-surfaced and plane it to the thickness you want.

The width of the wood for the body should not be less than 8½". You'll need some extra room to maneuver around as you make crosscuts and rip cuts, trim the edges and laminate the wood in the early stages.

SAWING THE WOOD

When you're satisfied with the thickness of the boards, get ready to make crosscuts for the body sections. Begin by sawing out the wood for the *middle* section. Each board, whether you're using two or three boards to make up the approximate thickness of 2" for the middle section, should be 24" long. When the boards have been sawed out, write either "M" or "Middle" on each board so they don't get mixed up with the other sections you're going to be sawing out. Put these boards aside for now.

Next, measure off six more boards 24" long. These boards will become the two *outer* sections, right and left, with each section being comprised of three boards glued together. Saw off these six lengths and place them in two stacks of three boards each. Mark these as well, with either an "R" for right or an "L" for left.

In order to avoid confusion and to keep the instructions from getting too kaleidoscopic, the instructions for the legs, head, neck and tail will be covered later. After you've read through the material once before starting on the project, you can choose to glue up as much of the wood as you wish at one time. By doing this you can save time by not having to go back and forth and repeating the same procedures all over again.

GLUING UP THE BODY SECTIONS

After the boards have been sawed out, it's time to glue them together to make up the three respective sections of the body. Although either yellow or white glue can be used for laminating the wood, yellow glue seems to be the stronger of the two. It also dries better in cooler temperatures. It's best to let the glue set up overnight so the boards are securely bonded together.

Begin by gluing together the boards for the middle body section. Place the boards adjacent to each other with the glue within easy reach. Also, keep a roll of paper towels nearby to wipe up excesses and spills. Squeeze glue onto the surfaces of the boards using a thin, flat piece of scrap wood

FIGURE 12 — *To achieve the correct thickness of the blanks, several pieces of wood are glued together before cutting out the pattern. This method of gluing up single pieces of wood to make a thicker piece is called laminating. A piece of scrap wood is used to spread glue evenly over the entire surface of the wood.*

to spread the glue on evenly and smoothly. Make sure both surfaces that come together are thoroughly covered with a thin application of glue. *(See Figure 12.)*

Later, after the glue dries, you'll have to trim the edge of the wood along one side. So try to keep the boards lined up as you place them together for clamping.

When the glue has been applied, begin securing the boards with clamps. *(See Figure 13.)* Start applying pressure in the middle of the

FIGURE 13 — *Clamps hold the laminated pieces of wood together until the glue dries. Keep a roll of paper towels handy to wipe off any excess glue that squeezes out from between the boards.*

boards so the glue is spread outward. Use a moderate amount of pressure until the glue begins to set. The boards will have a tendency to slide around as you're trying to clamp them, so wait a few minutes before applying more pressure. Use paper towels to wipe off excess glue.

Next, when the clamps are available again, glue up three of the boards you sawed off earlier to make up one of the outer body sections. Then, do the same with the remaining boards for the other body section.

Now that the wood is laminated, make an even, smooth surface along the length of one edge of the three sections. (The reason for trimming one edge is to establish a reference edge to place along the fence of a bandsaw later. A table saw could be used for the two outer sections when you get to that part of the procedure.) A jointer is at the top of the list for this trimming job, but you can also use a bench plane or a small power plane. Use whatever enables you to get one edge neatly trimmed on each of the three body sections.

ABOUT THE TEMPLATE PATTERN

The various parts of the horse pattern can be transferred to a sheet of paper or cardboard with tracing and carbon paper, or you can cut the parts out and place them onto the wood.(See pattern section in the back of this book.) If you'd like a more durable set of templates, trace the outline of each part onto ⅛" masonite. The broken lines shown on some of the horse parts represent the direction and depth for screw holes and/or dowel holes as described in detail further on in the instructions. Although it's obvious, for the most part, what each of the outlined parts represents, they're all number-coded in accordance with the following list:

1 – Left front leg
2 – Right front leg
3 – Right rear leg (Reverse lower part when joining)
4 – Left rear leg
5 – Two tail sections
6 – Front and back sections of saddle
7 – Head
8 – Neck
9 – Middle body section
10 – Right body section
11 – Left body section

Note: *The two-way arrows indicate the ideal direction of the wood grain.*

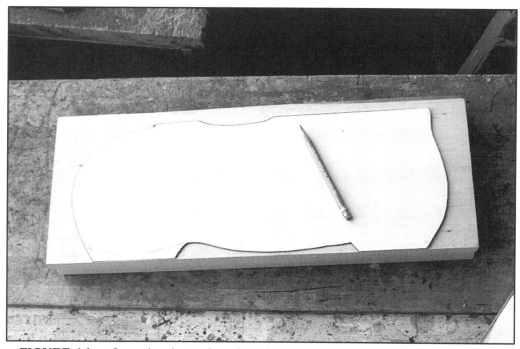

FIGURE 14 — *Once the glue is dry, place the pattern on the wood and trace around it with a pencil. Labeling the body pieces is a good idea; it may help to avoid confusion when assembling the blank later.*

TRANSFERRING THE BODY DESIGNS
TO THE WOOD

When each of the three sections has an evenly trimmed surface along one edge, copy the respective designs from the pattern sheet onto the laminated wood sections. *(See Figure 14.)*

On the two outer body sections, it doesn't matter whether you place the top or bottom edge of the templates against the trimmed edge of the wood. On the middle body section, the template should be positioned so that the neckline is flush against the trimmed edge, since there are no upper leg areas on this piece.

With a yard stick or other ruling implement, draw a line the length of each of the outer body sections, either at the top or bottom depending on how you've positioned the templates on the wood. The reason for these lines is to have the excess strip of wood, above or below the body outlines, marked and ready to be sawed off prior to sawing out the contours of the body sections, which is next on the agenda.

SAWING OUT THE BODY SECTIONS

Begin by sawing out the excess strip of wood from each of the two outer body sections. Use either a table saw or a bandsaw to make these thick rip cuts. (Small power tools and hand tools could conceivably be enlisted in a pinch.) If you're going to use a bandsaw, be sure to set up a fence on the table so there'll be a solid support against which the straight edge of

FIGURE 15 *— Use a bandsaw outfitted with a flexible blade to cut out the body pieces. These body pieces will also need to be laminated, so be sure to cut as close to the pattern lines as possible.*

the wood can be placed. Try to use a wide blade. If you end up with any raggedness along the edges from the bandsaw blade, plane these surfaces smooth before sawing out the contours of the body outlines.

A jointer, portable power plane or bench plane can be used to trim the edges. It's important to have smooth, straight surfaces along the edges on both outer body sections, because part of these surfaces are where the legs and the neck will ultimately be attached.

When you saw out the three body sections, try to use a flexible blade on the bandsaw, if possible. And try to stay close to the lines as you're sawing. *(See Figure 15.)*

When the three sections have been sawed out, stack them on top of each other, temporarily, in the order in which they'll be laminated into one unit. Take a look at how they line up with each other. Make pencil marks around any areas that have been undercut or otherwise don't conform to the way the other sections line up. Then, make adjustments by carefully trimming off the areas you've marked.

Pay close attention to the front upper leg area on the *right* body section. This surface is where the raised front leg of the horse will be attached. It's possible to use a jointer on this surface, but it's an awkward maneuver. If you're unaccustomed to using a jointer, it's not advisable that you attempt to plane the front surface in this way. However, if you are comfortable with a jointer, place the right outer body section on the "table" with the chest facing forward. The blade of the jointer should have a minimal setting, for instance $1/16$". This means you'll have to make several passes before any noticeable progress can be made. If a jointer is not available to you, use a belt/disc sander or a bench plane to even off the front upper leg surface.

GLUING THE BODY SECTIONS INTO ONE UNIT

It may help to avoid confusion if you mark "Right" or "R" and "Left" or "L" on the outer sections. Pencil in these designations on the surface of each section that will be facing outward, as opposed to the soon-to-be-glued inside surfaces. This may seem unnecessary to you, but sometimes distractions, tiredness or Mondays can result in the outer sections getting inadvertently reversed. Not a big problem, except the leg positions would be reversed for this design.

Set the middle body section down on top of the *inside* surface of one of the outer sections. Now, move the two sections (middle and one outer section) close to the edge of your work bench or table. Gather up the clamps you plan to use and, before applying glue, dry-clamp the wood. When you get ready to use the clamps for gluing, they will already be open to the width you'll need according to the width you used to dry-clamp the wood.

It's easier to laminate the body sections by gluing only two sections

FIGURE 16 — The body section of the carousel horse is made from three pattern cut-outs laminated together (a total of nine pieces of wood). Use a piece of scrap wood to spread glue evenly across the surface of the wood.

together first, and the remaining outer section later when the glue is thoroughly dry. *(See Figure 16.)*

Initially, the body sections will tend to slide out of place until the glue begins to set up. Starting with two sections will give you better control

FIGURE 17 — Clamps hold the laminated pieces of wood together as the glue dries. Try gluing two pieces together first and then add the third piece of wood. This two-step approach to laminating the thicker pieces of wood will keep the pieces from sliding out of place as the glue dries.

over the lamination of the wood. *(See Figure 17.)* The alternative is having to deal with three body sections at one time, as you wrestle with the clamps trying to keep the body in alignment. This can turn into a cliff-hanger as the glue begins to set.

Keep an eye on the glued-up sections for about ten minutes or so while the glue is still drying. If the wood begins to shift around, make adjustments by loosening the clamps, repositioning the body sections and tightening the clamps again. Wipe off the glue that is squeezed out as you apply more pressure with the clamps. This will cut down on the amount of hard droplets you'll have to deal with when the glue dries. The most crucial part of the alignment is at the top of the body. Keep the base of the neckline, where the neck will eventually be glued on, as evenly lined up across the three body sections as you possibly can. Lengthwise, be more concerned with keeping the front of the chest lined up, if you have to choose. Don't forget to follow the dry-clamping procedure as you prepare to glue on the remaining outer section. Although handscrews are shown in *Figure 18,* use whatever variety of clamps you can get your hands on. Apply as much evenly distributed pressure as possible.

FIGURE 18 — *Line up the edges of the laminated pieces as accurately as possible. Be sure to keep a close eye on the pieces during the first ten minutes of clamping; the pieces may shift before the glue starts to set up.*

When the glue has dried and the body is a single unit, direct your attention to the wide surface upon which the neck will be permanently attached. Additionally, take note of the small projecting strip of wood at the back of the saddle where the cantle will be glued. Make certain these surfaces are as smooth and flat as you can get them with the equipment you have to work with. It takes a jointer with at least an 8" capacity to be

FIGURE 19 — *Many larger woodworking shops may be equipped with a jointer. For the carousel horse, you'll need a jointer with a least an 8" capacity to smooth the flat edges of the laminated blank.*

able to surface the top of the body. *(See Figure 19.)* Unfortunately, the average small shop jointer is not that wide. You can try electric sanders, but you'll find they tend to leave uneven areas near the edges of flat surfaces. You might have luck with an upright stationary sander with a

FIGURE 20 — *If a jointer is unavailable, use a planer to smooth the flat edges. An upright stationary sander with a wide belt may also be used. Avoid electric sanders as they tend to leave uneven areas near the edges of flat surfaces.*

wide belt capacity. The best alternative is to manually plane the wide surface, as well as the narrower surface for the cantle at the back of the saddle. *(See Figure 20.)*

THE LEGS AND THE TAIL

Start by positioning the templates for the various leg parts and the tail on the surface of one of the boards you plan to use. Arrange the templates so that the arrows on each piece, representing the grain direction, are fairly parallel with the wood grain. Shift the template pieces around to get an idea of how you're going to work it out.

You don't have to get all the leg and tail parts on one length of wood. Make up as many combinations of boards as you'll need to get the parts of the legs and tail sawed out.

When you have a good idea of how much lumber will be required, remove the templates from the board, or boards, and begin gluing up the wood in threes the same way you did when laminating the body sections. The width of the legs and the tail parts should be approximately the same as that of the outer body sections (2⅝" give or take ⅛"). In fact, close is good enough. A slightly narrower or wider thickness won't make a significant difference.

After the boards have been laminated, draw the outlines of the various parts onto the wood. *(See Figure 21.)* Saw out the parts on the bandsaw. A flexible blade works best for this type of cutting. Make gross cuts, at first, then go back and cut around each part more carefully, sawing very

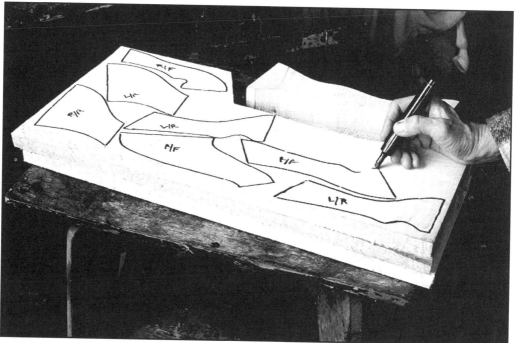

FIGURE 21 — *Laminate wood for the horse's legs and trace around the patterns. Cut out the pieces on a bandsaw, first making rough cuts to separate the pieces and then returning to saw along the lines.*

close to the pencil marks. The exceptions on each part are the straight lines that represent the flat areas that will have to be joined to matching parts. These saw cuts should be made just outside the lines to leave a slight margin for finer surfacing. Leave a slight margin on the hooves as well.

The straight edges on these parts, indicated by the straight lines, need to be surfaced so they're as smooth and even as the edges that you made on the body sections. As mentioned earlier, a wide-belt sander can be used with some success to smooth edges, especially on smaller areas.

Instructions for drilling the holes and binding together these various parts, as well as other parts of the horse, will be forthcoming after the remaining parts that need to be laminated and surfaced have been covered.

THE NECK

The neck should be about 3¾" to 4" in thickness. Don't be concerned if the thickness you end up with is a bit over, you can always carve it down.

Begin by placing the neck template on one end of the 10" wide board. Position the template so the arrow is pointing in the same direction as the grain. This means that the template will be at a cockeyed angle on the board. Draw a line across the width of the board to establish the length of this first section. Don't be too exact, leave a little room for cutting error. Mark off four or five additional sections, or as many as you'll need based on the net thickness of the board with which you're working.

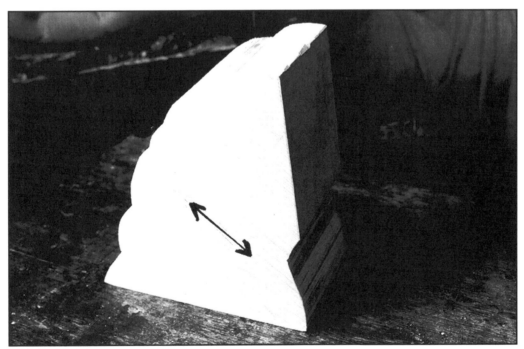

FIGURE 22 — *Cut out the neck, making sure that the arrow on the pattern follows the direction of the wood grain. The pattern will need to be angled slightly on the laminated wood to accommodate the grain.*

Saw off the neck sections and glue and clamp them together following the procedures you used on previous laminations. When the glue dries, draw the outline of the neck onto the block of wood. Saw out the neck on the bandsaw. It should end up looking something like the example shown in *Figure 22.*

Make the two flat surfaces smooth by using a wide-belt electric sander or a hand plane. It's not a good idea to use a jointer due to the odd angle of the grain in relation to the straight edges. More than likely pieces of wood would split off.

THE HEAD

The block of wood for the head should be approximately 3¾" in thickness, which may be slightly thinner than the neck, depending on any variations in thickness of the boards you glue together.

Start by placing the head template on one end of the board you're going to use, unless you're making the head from scraps left over from previous cuts. Measure off the lengths you'll need to collectively make up the thickness of the head. Saw off the individual lengths of wood. Before you glue and clamp the pieces into one solid block, place them together. Establish an even surface along one edge of the combined block. This surface (after the wood has been laminated) will become the bottom surface of the head. Criss-cross the bottom with a pencil so you'll have a reference mark when you reassemble the wood and glue it into one block.

Next, glue the pieces together. When the glue dries, run the bottom surface of the block across a jointer or hand-plane it until it's perfectly

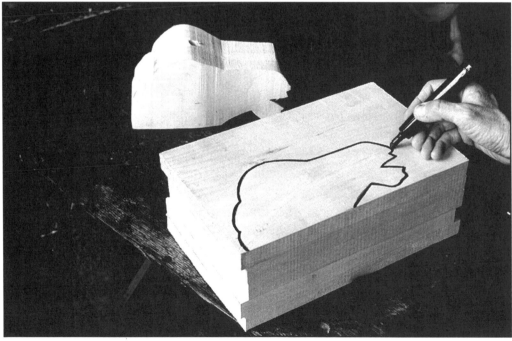

FIGURE 23 — *Trace the head pattern onto a piece of laminated wood. Use a jointer, sander or planer to smooth the flat edge of the wood.*

flat. Then, place the head template against the side of the block of wood. Draw around the outline of the head as shown in the photograph. *(See Figure 23.)*

THE FRONT AND BACK OF THE SADDLE

The front and back sections of the saddle, the pommel and cantle respectively, can be glued up from miscellaneous leftover scraps of wood. Because these sections are so small, try to saw them out of the same laminated piece of wood. *(See Figure 24.)* Glue together enough wood to

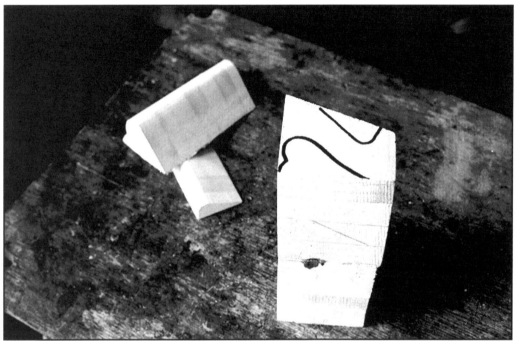

FIGURE 24 — *Cutting out the pommel and the cantle with a bandsaw can be difficult and dangerous because of the small sizes of the pieces. As an alternative, glue a few pieces of scrap wood to the horse and use hand tools to shape these two pieces.*

make up a total width that is close to the width of the body. It's more important for the cantle to be wide than it is for the pommel. In fact, the piece for the pommel only needs to be about 4" or 5" across. The pommel will eventually become very narrow compared to the cantle, which will remain fairly wide. Since there's a good possibility that you'll opt to drill a 1" diameter hole through the front area of the saddle for a pole, later, the pommel can even be left off. Or, it can be left off for now and be created later by building up a small mound using a good wood filler. (More about wood filler later in the text.)

If you plan on sawing out these sections on a bandsaw be *extremely* careful. Keep your fingers a healthy distance from the unforgiving saw blade. The refining of the contours and flat surfaces can be done on an electric sander.

An alternate and infinitely safer way to make a cantle and pommel is to simply cut out a few short, narrow pieces from the scraps and glue them onto the body without sawing out the curves shown on the template and in the photographs. You can glue two pieces on top of one another to make a cantle and use one piece of wood for a pommel. Make sure each piece is wide enough and that the grain is going in the same direction as the grain on the body. Later, after the pieces have been glued to the body, you can remove a notch of wood from along the back of the cantle with a hand saw. Then, do some rough filing with a rasp. In this way, you can create whatever contours you desire for the saddle, using carving tools for the refinements. And you'll avoid any hazards that can and do occur working close to the blade of a bandsaw.

GLUING THE LEG PARTS TOGETHER

Begin by matching up the three pairs of leg parts that need to be permanently joined. Next, saw off three 1" long pegs from a ½" diameter dowel, or use ½" diameter pre-cut, fluted dowel pins. Put all but one of the dowel pegs aside. Choose one set of leg parts from the three sets to be glued together.

Use an awl to punch a starter hole in the center of the flat surface on one half of the leg. (It doesn't matter whether you start with the top or bottom half of the leg.) Insert a ½" diameter spade bit in your drill and drill down about a half inch into the surface of the leg. (See Figure 25.) Then, insert a ½" diameter metal dowel center into the hole. (See Figure 26.) Place the two halves of the leg together, line them up and tap one end of the leg with a mallet.

FIGURE 25 — *Dowels will help to hold the legs together. First, drill a hole, ½" in diameter and ½" deep, into the surface of the leg.*

FIGURE 26 — *Next insert a ½" diameter metal dowel center into the hole. Place the two halves of the leg together and tap one end gently with a mallet. Using the indentation made be the metal dowel center as a guide, drill another hole, ½" in diameter and ½" deep, in the other half of the leg.*

Drill a ¹/₂" diameter hole about a half inch deep into the flat surface of the other half of the leg, using the tiny hole left by the dowel center as a starting hole. Next, put a dowel peg into one of the two holes. (See

FIGURE 27 — *To check the fit, push the dowel into one of the holes and then push the two leg pieces together. Do not glue the pieces together at this time. Minor discrepancies in the fit can be filled in with glue or filler; major discrepancies call for the holes to be plugged and redrilled.*

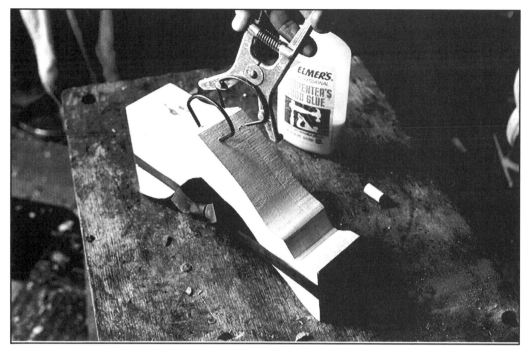

FIGURE 28 — *Spring miter clamps and a strip of tire tube hold the leg pieces together as the glue dries.*

Figure 27.) Press the two halves of the leg together, but do not glue them yet.

A few spring miter clamps and a strip of tire tube tied into a small band can be used to hold the two parts together. *(See Figure 28.)* Try dry-clamping this combination before applying glue. These procedures should

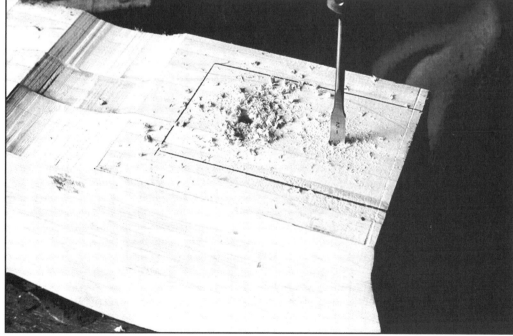

FIGURE 29 — *Dowels are also used to hold the neck section to the body. Drill two holes, 1/2" in diameter and 3/4" deep in the body.*

FIGURE 30 — *Place a ½″ diameter metal dowel center in each of the holes.*

be used on the two remaining pairs of leg parts that also need to be joined together.

GLUING THE NECK TO THE BODY

Draw a center line, lengthwise, along the flat surface of the body where the neck will be attached. Then, place the bottom of the neck on this surface. Draw a line around the bottom of the neck onto the surface. Remove the neck. Measure in about $1\frac{1}{2}$″ or more from the center line at the front of the body and mark the spot. Now measure in the same distance from the back and make another mark. Punch each mark with the awl, then drill a $\frac{1}{2}$″ diameter hole about $\frac{3}{4}$″ deep into each punch hole. *(See Figure 29.)*

Insert a $\frac{1}{2}$″ diameter metal dowel center into each of the holes. *(See Figure 30.)* Place the neck onto the rectangular area on the body again. Give the top of the neck a tap with a mallet. *(See Figure 31.)* Remove the neck and turn it over. Drill a $\frac{1}{2}$″ diameter hole into the two impressions left in the bottom of the neck. *(See Figure 32.)*

Next, insert two $\frac{1}{2}$″ dowel pegs each about $1\frac{1}{4}$″ long, into the holes and press the neck onto the body. Make any adjustments necessary, at this point, with the help of the hand drill.

You'll need two bar clamps to secure the neck to the body. In addition, you'll need a third clamp of some kind to hold the body to the bench or table top. A quick-action adjustable clamp, or a band clamp, can be used to secure the body while you set up the bar clamps. Make use of any other clamps you own or can borrow that open up to the width needed to hold the body securely to your work surface.

If you're going to use metal clamps, place thin wood scraps between the metal plates and the surface of the wood before tightening the clamps. The wood scraps will serve as protective cushioning to prevent damage to the wood, in particular to the flat surfaces where the front legs will be joined to the body. It's important that you go through all the motions of clamping the neck to the body before actually applying the glue.

After you've tried out the clamping arrangement, remove the neck and pull out the dowel pegs. Open the clamps, band belts and whatever else you're planning to use to a slightly

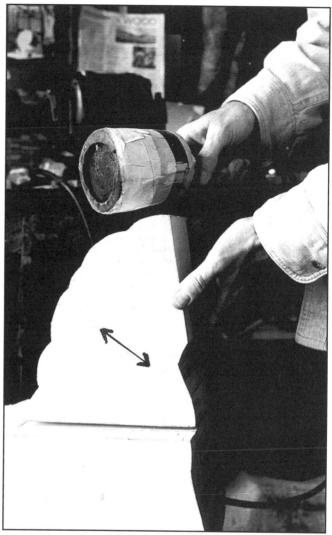

FIGURE 31 — *Hold the neck section in place and gently tap the wood with a mallet.*

larger width than what you'll really need. This will keep you from having to make adjustments after the glue has been applied.

When everything is in place, spread the glue evenly within the rectangular area on top of the body. Do the same with the underside of the neck. Also, squeeze a few drops of glue into the holes. Rub glue around on the two dowel pegs as well, but not too much. Insert the dowel pegs into the two holes in the top of the body, then place the neck over the pegs and begin clamping. *(See Figure 33.)*

GLUING ON THE SADDLE PARTS

When the neck and body have been permanently attached, glue the cantle and pommel to the top of the body. It's better to use band belts or strips of tire tubes to secure these parts as the glue is drying. The wood pieces are too fragile for metal clamps to be used. As you've probably already observed, there's not much room behind the neck for a pommel,

FIGURE 32 — *Using the indentations left by the metal dowel centers as guides, drill two more holes, ½" in diameter and ¾" deep, in the body. Insert dowels and check the fit.*

let alone a pole later on. Just do the best you can in that area. (On some of the original carousel horses, the pole went right through the pommel, while on others a pommel was not to be found. At least not one that actually projected up significantly from the saddle. Instead, there would sometimes be a short flat area or a small barely detectable mound. So if there isn't much room to maneuver, take it with a grain of salt.)

If you're going to use strips of tire tubes as band clamps, cut the strips into a few different lengths beforehand. It's better to have several lengths to choose from according to the tension required. Criss-cross the tire tube strips around the body and over the saddle part that you're gluing. *(See Figure 34.)* Keep an eye on the cantle (or pommel) until the glue becomes less slippery.

TEMPORARILY ATTACHING THE LEGS TO THE BODY

The tools and materials needed to drill the holes in the legs and temporarily attach them to the body are as follows: an electric hand drill; a ½" diameter spade bit; a $^{13}/_{64}$" diameter twist bit; a ⅛" diameter twist bit; two 2" and two 2½" #10 roundhead screws; an awl and a screwdriver. Oh yes, and one more thing. A ⅛" diameter twist bit that is six inches in length. Although this extra long twist bit is for use later in drilling through the head and into the neck, it may come in handy for drilling into the

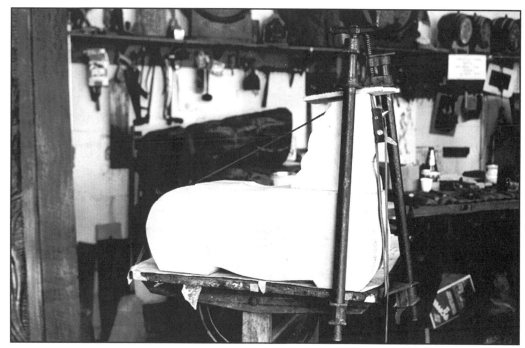

FIGURE 33 — *To avoid too many adjustments to the clamps after the glue has been applied, dry-clamp the neck section to the body before applying the glue. Once the clamps have been adjusted, open them slightly, remove the blank, apply glue to the two sections, and reclamp the wood.*

back legs, as you will see shortly. This type of long bit is available at most independent hardware stores and possibly some of the better stocked franchise hardware stores.

Start by placing one of the leg templates against its wood counter-

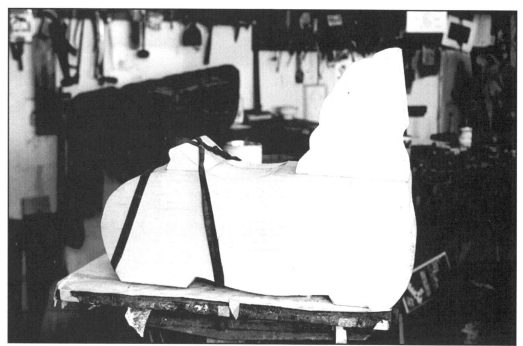

FIGURE 34 — *The tubes criss-crossed over the cantle keep the cantle in place as the glue dries. This same clamping method works well for the pommel also.*

FIGURE 35 — *The legs are secured to the body with dowels and screws. To make the holes for the dowels, hold the leg against the body and mark the angle of the drill hole on the side of the wood. Using that mark as a guide, drill a hole, ½" in diameter and ½" deep in the leg.*

part. Move the straight edge of the template down an inch or so from the straight edge of the wood and draw a line on the leg indicating the angle for the dowel hole. Remove the template and go over the line

FIGURE 36 — *To make a matching hole in the body, place a ½" diameter metal dowel center in the hole in the leg. Hold the leg against the body and tap the leg gently with a mallet. Use the indentation left by the metal dowel center as a guide to drill the hole in the body. Insert a dowel and check the fit.*

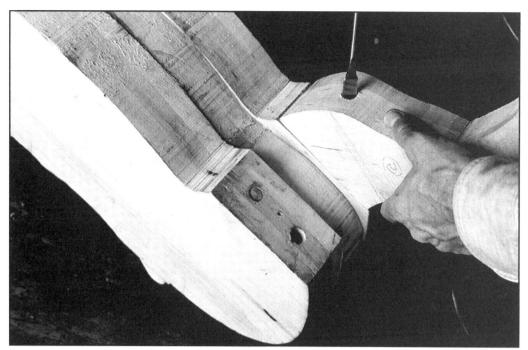

FIGURE 37 — *Drill holes for the screws, one in each leg. Start by drilling a ½" diameter hole in the leg.*

more emphatically so it's easy to see as you're drilling. *(See Figure 35.)*

Make a punch hole with the awl into the top surface of the leg you're working on in accordance with the line you drew on the side. Drill down about a half-inch into the top of the leg at the point where you made a punch hole.

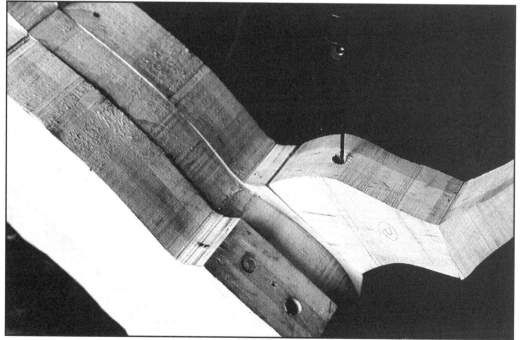

FIGURE 38 — *Use a ⅛" twist bit and a 13⁄64" twist bit to extend the hole through the leg section and into the body.*

Next, insert a ½" metal dowel center in the hole in the leg. Turn the body upside down and place the leg on the matching upper leg section. Tap the bottom of the leg to make a punch hole in the flat surface on the body. Drill a ½" diameter hole in the upper leg section. *(See Figure 36.)* Drill down about a half inch just as you did with the leg. Follow these procedures on the other three legs.

Insert a dowel peg into each of the holes and fit the legs temporarily onto the upper leg sections. Use the hand drill to adjust any off-center problems by widening or deepening the holes, as the situation calls for.

The holes for the screws are next; one screw for each leg. The object is to drill a ½" diameter hole in the legs first, using the templates as guides. Then, drill a ⅛" diameter hole through the bottom center of the first hole. The small hole will be where the screw will go in each leg, and the large hole will be where a dowel peg goes to conceal the screw and plug the hole. The peg should be inserted after you've finished carving the horse.

Begin by marking on the side of each leg the approximate angle and depth for the screw hole. Use the reference marks on the leg templates as guides. Then, make a punch mark at the point indicated on each leg where the hole will be drilled. Drill a ½" diameter hole into each leg. *(See Figure 37.)* It isn't necessary to hold the legs against the respective upper body section to drill the holes. Follow the marks you made to get the correct angle and depth needed.

When the ½" diameter holes have been drilled, insert a ⅛" twist bit in the drill. Start with one of the front legs by placing the bit into the ½"

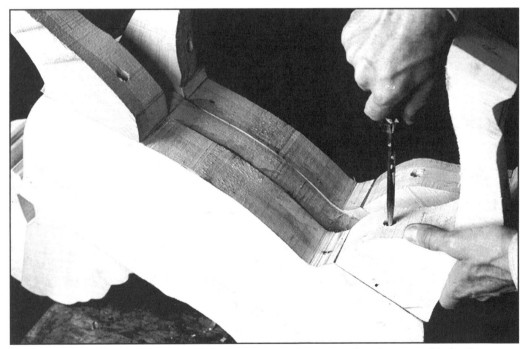

FIGURE 39 — *Secure the legs to the body with #10 round head screws. Slight discrepancies in the fit can be corrected with glue or filler. If the discrepancies are significant, plug the holes with dowels and redrill.*

diameter hole. Probe around until you find the tiny hole left by the tip of the spade bit. Drill through the hole into the upper leg section. Do the same thing with the other legs.

The back legs will probably require you to use the extra long $\frac{1}{8}$" twist bit, depending on the angle and depth of the holes you drilled. *(See Figure 38.)* Drill deeply enough into each of the four legs to accommodate the threaded part of the screws.

Now, replace the $\frac{1}{8}$" twist bit with a $\frac{13}{64}$" twist bit. This bit will be used to enlarge the $\frac{1}{8}$" diameter hole in the legs so the shank of the screw will easily pass through the hole.

Insert the $\frac{13}{64}$" bit into the exit hole of the leg. In other words, start from the flat surface and drill in the opposite direction from which you drilled the original hole through the leg. Run the bit back and forth a few times to clean the hole.

When all the holes have been drilled, temporarily secure each leg to the body using the #10 round head screws. *(See Figure 39.)* More than likely, you'll need $2\frac{1}{2}$" screws for the back legs. Each leg should fit relatively flush against the upper leg sections. If there is a slight imperfection in the match-up, a few extra gobs of glue will take up the slack later. If there's a significant discrepancy in the way the leg fits against the body, you'd better evaluate the situation. Possibly additional planing or sanding will take care of it. If not, you might have to go through the process of putting together another leg, especially if the problem is due to the way the leg was cut out.

Should you run into any problems with the holes in the legs that

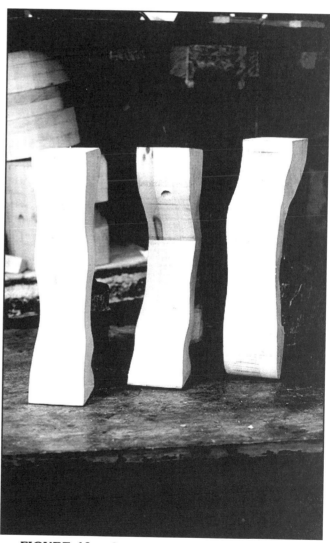

FIGURE 40 — *Sawing out the basic contours of the legs is an optional but helpful step. Draw guidelines just inside the edge of the leg and saw off the extra wood.*

FIGURE 41 — *Hold the pattern against the head and use a pencil to mark the position of the eye.*

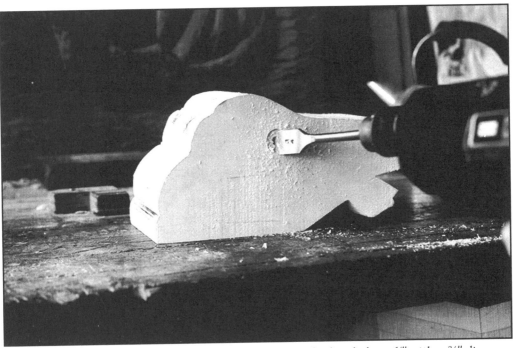

FIGURE 42 — *Leaning the drill forward, drill into the head about ½" with a ¾" diameter spade bit.*

seem to be beyond repair, plug up the holes with dowel pegs. Rub glue on the dowels before inserting them into the holes. After the glue dries start over by drilling new holes adjacent to the old ones.

Before moving on to the head, consider sawing out basic contours on both sides of each leg. This minimal shaping can be done by first drawing guidelines just inside the edges of each leg, then sawing out the waste wood. These basic contours will allow you to see how the shape of each leg will evolve as you begin carving. *(See Figure 40.)* It is not absolutely necessary that you shape the legs as described, but it does help.

GETTING STARTED ON THE HEAD

Before drilling the holes for temporarily attaching the head to the neck, saw out on the bandsaw some of the excess wood on each side of the head to make basic contours. Even a little basic shaping will help you to better visualize what direction you'll be heading in as the carving gets underway. (Refer to *Figure 43* to get an idea of the shaping on the head.)

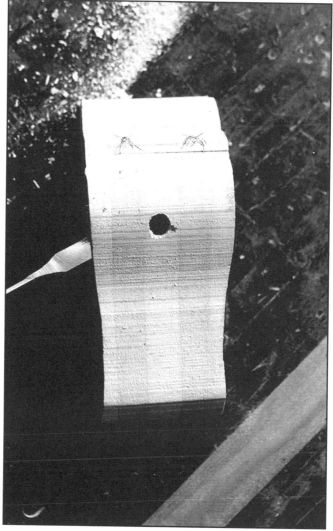

FIGURE 43 — *Depth adjustments to the eye hole can be made once the head is closer to being finished.*

Don't worry about exact measurements for this crude initial shaping. Just remove enough wood from the sides to establish the basic shape. Draw in guidelines before sawing along each side of the head. Try to make the contoured lines as evenly matched as you can.

Next, place the head template against the side of the head and draw a circle around the eye hole. *(See Figure 41.)* And, while you're holding the template in place, draw guidelines for the ears close to the top of the head to indicate where the ear holes will be drilled (after you've drilled the eye holes).

Make a punch hole in the center of the eye circle on one side of the head. Begin drilling into the circle using a $3/4$" diameter spade bit. *(See Figure 42.)* Lean the wood bit forward at approximately a 350° angle. *(See Figure 43.)* Drill in about a half inch. Make any depth adjustments later, after you've made considerable progress in carving the entire head.

EARS AND EAR HOLES

FIGURE 44 — *Draw guidelines on the top of the head for the placement of the ears. Drill two holes, ½" deep, into the head. Be sure both holes are drilled at the same angle.*

Draw guidelines on top of each side of the head to show exactly where it is you are going to drill the ear holes. Do this by placing the flat side of the 1⅛" diameter spade bit, or whatever diameter bit you decide to use, on top of the head. *(See Figure 44.)*

Make two punch marks with your awl to indicate where to begin drilling the ear holes. Drill the holes down into the head about a ½" deep. Drill both holes at the same angle.

There are a few ways to make the two cylindrical ear pieces which will eventually be carved and glued into the ear holes. First, if you have access to a lathe you can make a 1⅛" dowel by turning a length of scrap wood from one of the leftover pieces. The dimensions of the wood should be approximately 1½" x 1½" x 6". As you turn the wood into a cylindrical shape, use calipers to control the diameter. (For comments regarding ears carved from dowels, refer to the last paragraph on page XX in the workbook.) Making a dowel out of the same wood from which the rest of the horse is made will allow for a consistency throughout the carving.

An alternative to making the ear pieces yourself is to purchase a dowel at a hardware store. The problem is that store-bought dowels may not be available in the size you want. On the other hand, if you should buy a slightly larger diameter dowel you can always carve some wood from the end that gets inserted into the ear hole. Or, you can simply drill 1" diameter holes in the head and use a 1" diameter dowel for the ears. One last thought on store-bought dowels is that they're often made of

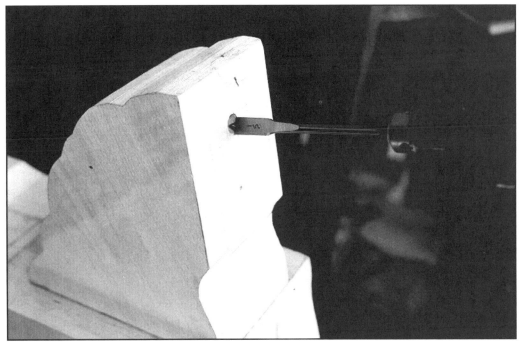

FIGURE 45 — *Attach the head with a dowel peg and a roundhead screw. To position the pegs, first drill a hole, ½" in diameter and ¾" deep, in the neck.*

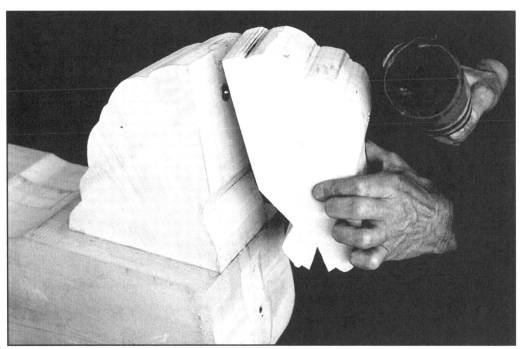

FIGURE 46 — *Next, place a ½" diameter metal dowel center in the hole. Hold the head in place and tap it gently with a mallet.*

wood that is either inferior to carve (such as fir) or much harder than the wood with which you're working (such as maple). Some hardware stores carry dowels made of soft pine, rather than the standard harder dowels, but not all hardware and lumber outlets carry them.

If you don't plan to use a lathe to make a dowel piece for ears, nor want to buy a dowel at a hardware store, you can just saw out a length of wood

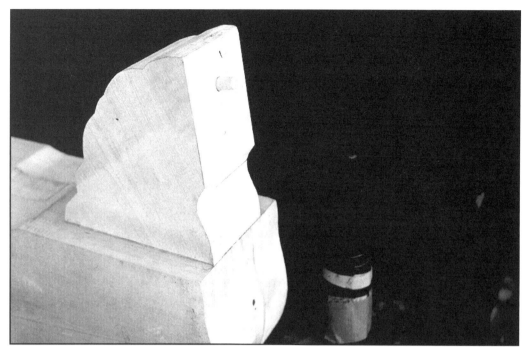

FIGURE 47 — *Using the indentation left by the metal dowel center, drill a hole in the head, ½" in diameter and ¾" deep. Insert the dowel and fit the pieces together.*

based generally on the dimensions mentioned above. When the wood is sawed out, draw a circle on each end equal to the diameter of the ear holes. The circles will serve as references as you carve the wood into a rough-shaped dowel. When the length of wood begins to take on a cylindrical shape, alternate the carving by using a rasp and medium-grit sandpaper to

FIGURE 48 — *Once the neck and the head pieces fit together snugly, remove the head and make a mark on the outside of the head to indicate the angle of the screw. Use a ½" diameter spade bit to drill the first part of the hole.*

smooth off the surface. It isn't necessary that you make a perfectly round cylinder the entire length of the wood. It is important, however, that you make one end of each ear piece, after the wood is sawed in half, the same diameter as the holes into which they'll be inserted.

TEMPORARILY ATTACHING THE HEAD TO THE NECK

The head is attached to the neck with a dowel peg and a roundhead screw, just as you did with the legs. First, punch a starter hole in the flat surface of the neck approximately $1\frac{1}{2}$" down from the top. Then, drill a $\frac{1}{2}$" diameter hole about $\frac{3}{4}$" deep into the neck. *(See Figure 45.)* Insert a $\frac{1}{2}$" metal dowel center into the hole. Place the head against the neck and tap it gently with your mallet. *(See Figure 46.)* Remove the head and turn it upside down.

Drill a $\frac{1}{2}$" diameter hole about $\frac{1}{2}$" deep into the underside of the head where the metal spike left a mark. Next, saw off a $1\frac{1}{4}$" long peg from a $\frac{1}{2}$" diameter dowel and insert it into the hole in the neck. *(See Figure 47.)* Place the head onto the neck. If no adjustments are needed, remove the head and get ready to drill the hole in the head for the screw.

The method of drilling the hole in the head for the 3" #10 roundhead screw is the same as that used to drill the screw holes in the legs. A large diameter hole is drilled first, followed by a smaller diameter hole. Use the markings on the head template, which you can transfer to the wood, as a guide to eyeball the direction of the hole to be drilled through the head.

Draw a straight line down one side of the head parallel to the shaft for the screw shown on the tem-

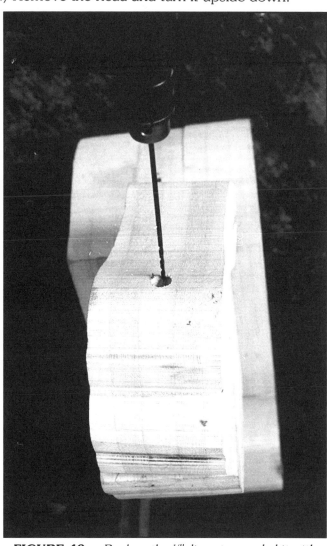

FIGURE 49 — *Replace the $\frac{1}{2}$" diameter spade bit with a six-inch-long $\frac{1}{8}$" diameter twist bit. Join the head and the neck and continue drilling the hole, first with the $\frac{1}{8}$" diameter twist bit and then with a $\frac{13}{64}$" diameter twist bit.*

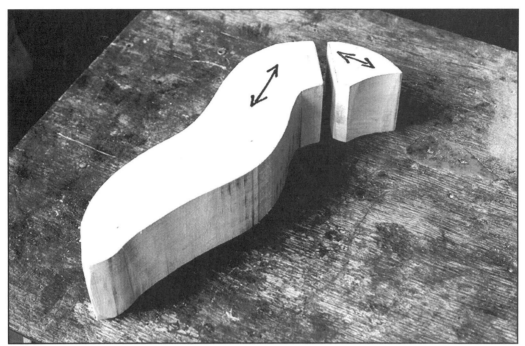

FIGURE 50 — *Align the arrows with the grain of the wood and cut out the tail. Drill ½" diameter holes for dowel pegs, apply glue and clamp the tail pieces with spring miter*

plate. This line will indicate the direction the screw will travel when it's inserted into the head and, subsequently, the neck. By staying close to the guidelines as you drill, you'll wind up with enough distance between the screw hole and the hole for the dowel so the two holes will not have inter-

FIGURE 51 — *Hold the tail against the rump and mark its position. Drill a hole, ½" in diameter and 1" deep into the rump. Place a ½" diameter metal dowel center in the hole, hold the tail in place and gently tap it with a mallet. Use the indentation left by the metal dowel center as a guide for drilling a hole in the tail, ½" in diameter and ½" deep.*

sected (where they both exit). This is a happy thing, because it will mean you won't have to plug up one or both of the holes and give it another go.

The head should be placed on your work surface as you get ready to drill the hole. The starting point for drilling the screw hole is in the middle of the head at the top. Make a punch mark with the awl on top of the head in relation to the guideline you've drawn on one side of the head.

Before you begin to drill, hold the $\frac{1}{2}$" diameter spade bit against the side of the head to gauge how much room you'll need near the bottom of the head for the shank of the screw to pass through. Tear off a small piece of masking tape, electricians tape or elastic bandage and use it as a stop guide on the shank of the bit so you'll know when you've drilled down far enough. Then, drill down through the head with the $\frac{1}{2}$" diameter spade bit. Stay parallel with the line alongside the head. *(See Figure 48.)*

When the stop guide is level with the top of the head, you've drilled far enough. Run the drill bit back and forth a few times to clean the hole of loose fibers.

Replace the $\frac{1}{2}$" diameter spade bit with the six inch long $\frac{1}{8}$" diameter twist bit. Then, insert the dowel peg in the neck again, and temporarily join the head to the neck. When the neck is positioned where you want it to be, meaning in a straight line with the rest of the body or at a *very slight* angle to the (horse's) right, probe around in the $\frac{1}{2}$" diameter hole in the head until you find the small hole left by the tip of the spade bit. Drill the rest of the way through the head into the neck with the long twist bit. There's no need to drill deeply right now, just enough to start the hole. *(See Figure 49.)*

Remove the head, then replace the long bit with a $\frac{13}{64}$" diameter twist bit. Turn the head upside down and run the bit into the screw hole several times to make a clean hole. This enlarged diameter hole will provide the correct clearance necessary for the shank of the long screw.

Replace the $\frac{13}{64}$" bit with the standard length $\frac{1}{8}$" twist bit. The shorter bit will be more stable and easier to control. Remove the head and drill about $1\frac{3}{4}$" deep into the neck.

PUTTING THE TAIL TOGETHER

Saw out the two pieces for the tail from the laminated boards used for the legs or from other leftover scraps of wood. Both surfaces of the wood where the tail will be joined into one unit have to be as smooth and even as the surfaces were for the pairs of legs. *(See Figure 50.)*

Glue the tail pieces together using the same procedures as when you joined the leg parts. This includes drilling the holes for a dowel peg before applying glue, and using spring clamps and a strip of tire tube to hold the parts together after the glue is applied. (Be sure to make a dry run with the clamping apparatuses before you put the glue on.)

When the tail is glued together, hold it up against the rump and mark off the position you'd like it to be in when it's attached to the body.

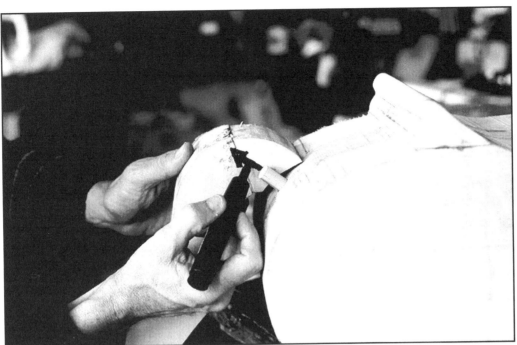

FIGURE 52 — *To make sure the angles of both holes are the same, hold the tail in place beside the dowel peg and draw an arrow on the tail to indicate the angle of the hole. Match the angle of the bit to the angle of this mark as you drill the hole.*

Drill a ½" diameter hole about 1" deep into the middle of the rump, according to where you made a reference mark. *(See Figure 51.)* Next, insert the ½" metal dowel center into the hole in the rump. Hold the tail in place against the rump and give it a tap. Then, saw off a ½" diameter peg approximately 1½" long. Insert the peg into the rump and hold the tail in position against the rump, but to one side of the peg. *(See Figure 52.)*

Draw a line on the side of the tail indicating the intended angle. When you start to drill, eyeball the line so the angle of the hole will parallel the angle of the dowel peg sticking out of the rump. If a minor adjustment is needed for a better fit, roll the spade bit around in each of the holes until the two pieces line up better.

PUTTING IT ALL TOGETHER

Temporarily assemble the horse blank utilizing all the dowel pegs and screws required to attach the various parts. Stand the horse up to make sure it's relatively level. If there is any noticeable unevenness, use a sander to make adjustments to the bottom of the hooves. Any major discrepancy due to initial overcutting or oversanding of one or more of the leg parts may require that you put together a replacement leg from whatever scraps remain.

Remember, the head, tail and legs should not be glued to the body until you're through carving and sanding. The reason will become very clear as you browse through the rest of the book. A photograph of the assembled horse blank can be found on page 18, Figure 11.

♞ *CHAPTER III* ♞

GETTING STARTED

Begin by clamping the body of the horse to the edge of a work bench or work table. The body should be placed on its side with the belly facing out toward you. Use a large deep gouge or a sharp draw knife to carve off the edges around the lower part of the body, including the area around the upper legs. Don't try to take off too much wood on one pass. *(See Figures 53-1 and 53-2.)* A draw knife will quickly and efficiently carve off the edges around the body, which includes the rump area when you get to it. But don't feel compelled to use one. Some people take a long time getting the hang of using a draw knife and ultimately feel more comfortable chugging and chunking along with gouges. At any rate, try not to force the wood with whatever tools you'll be using to do the initial carving. If the wood wants to split off, approach it from the opposite direction. Maneuver around until you feel the wood yielding more smoothly.

FIGURE 53-1 — *Clamp the body to a work bench and use a large gouge to remove wood from the lower part of the body.*

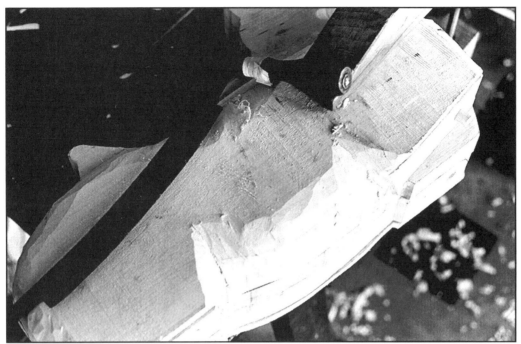

FIGURE 53-2 — *A draw knife may also be used to remove wood from the lower part of the body.*

Now rotate the body around, *not over*, so the upper part of the horse faces outward. Again, remove wood from around the edges. A little rounding off will be sufficient for now, not too much. *(See Figure 54.)* Start chunking away the wood that juts out along the shoulder line where the neck is joined to the body. Begin establishing the downward curve of the shoulder. *(See Figure 55.)* The objective is for you to get acquainted

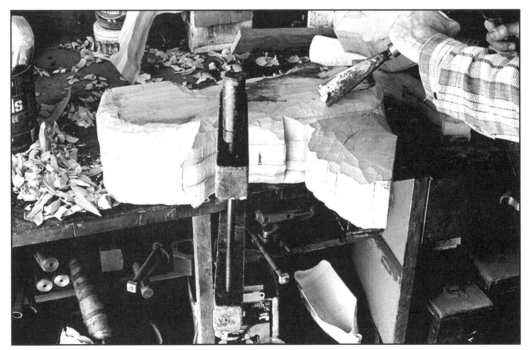

FIGURE 54 — *Turn the body around and continue removing wood from the edges.*

FIGURE 55 — Remove wood from the shoulder line where the neck is joined to the body. Begin to establish the downward curve of the shoulder.

with the texture of the wood at the same time you're carving out the rough shape of the body.

When you feel as though you're not sure if you should stop or go on, stop. Turn the body *over* and repeat on the other side what you just finished doing on the first side. *(See Figures 56-1, 56-2 and 56-3.)* After

FIGURES 56-1, 56-2 AND 56-3 — Turn the body over and remove wood from the other side of the horse. Remove approximately the same amount of wood from each side. (Figures 56-2 and 56-3 follow on next page.)

you've carved off approximately the same amount of wood, put the body aside for awhile. It's time to get started on the legs.

CLAMPING DOWN THE LEGS

One way to secure the legs while you carve them is to use an adjustable handclamp (handscrew). You can place the leg you're carving on its side, then clamp it directly to the work surface.

An alternative method is to set the clamp down flat and position the leg in the jaws of the clamp the way you want it. Tighten the jaws, then

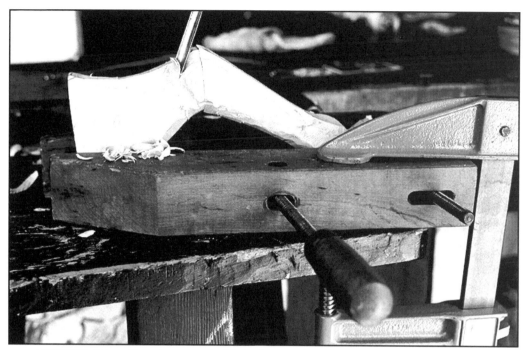

FIGURE 57 — *Use clamps to hold the leg in place during carving. The leg can be clamped directly to a work bench or clamped inside a second set of clamps that will hold it securely to the table.*

secure that clamp to the bench or table with a second clamp, or bar clamp or C-clamp—whatever holds it secure as you are carving. *(See Figure 57.)*

No matter which way you clamp the legs, after a certain amount of time they're going to become awkward and more fragile to deal with. There seems to be no getting around it. The gadget described on pages 14 and 15 (Figures 7,8, and 9) will help you considerably when carving the legs after you rough-shape them.

ROUGH-SHAPING THE FRONT LEGS

The only difference between the two front legs is in the positioning, as a result of the slightly raised right leg. Since this difference is not extreme, the instructions for carving both front legs will be presented as one, for the most part. This singular description format will also be used for the instructions on the back legs. The following information and the accompanying photographs should be enough to get you well into the carving.

Begin by trimming off the edges of the front leg from top to bottom, using either a medium shallow gouge or a draw knife. Don't take off too much, just enough to get a feel of things as you round off the sharp edges. After you finish the initial removal of wood, giving the leg a crude roundness, pencil in an oval shape on the top flat surface of the leg where it will join the body. The oval shape should be drawn fairly close to the edge of the wood. This mark will serve as a guideline to give you an idea

FIGURE 58 — *Using a shallow medium gouge or a draw knife, remove small amounts of wood from the legs to give them a general shape. Mark off the area at the top of the right front leg with a pencil. This area should not be carved until the finishing stage.*

of how far in you should carve the upper part of the leg, near the top. (Refer ahead to *Figure 29* in this chapter.)

The exception is the right front leg. Don't do anything rash to the inside area where the leg, at the top, lies flat against the body. In fact, hold the raised leg in place on the body and, with a dark-leaded pencil, draw a line along the inside of the top of the leg where it meets the body. *(See Figure 58.)* This line will remind you not to carve the flat upper area of the leg. (When you reach the finishing stage, you'll be glad you left this patch of wood alone.)

Next, draw circles on the front and both sides of the knee area where the knob of the knee will emerge. *(See Figure 59.)* Also, make circles to show where the fetlock will be carved. As the circles are carved off, draw on new ones. They will help you keep your bearings until the contours begin to appear on the leg. The object is to remove just enough wood, for now, to suggest the shape of the knee, fetlock and the coronet-hoof.

Do not carve the leg to near completion with all kinds of finely shaped details; it's too early for that. Periodically, step back and observe your progress from both the front and side to see that things are kept relatively balanced as you carve. Before getting into more detailed carving, here's a capsule review of the leg.

On the outside of the upper leg there is a long bulge of muscle. This bulge should be tapered and subtle, rather than swelled out in an exaggerated manner. The knee should be rounded, initially, yet slightly flattened out on the sides. The knee then tapers into the cannon, which is the area between the knee and the fetlock. The fetlock balloons out, then curves in at the pastern, which is a narrow cylindrical-shaped section of the lower leg between the fetlock and the coronet. The area called the coronet flares out just below the pastern and overhangs the hoof. Last but not least is the hoof. *(See Figure 60.)*

Try to keep the pastern from getting too thin. It should be in relative proportion to the thickness of the leg above the fetlock (the cannon). One way to control the shaping of the pastern is to use a piece of rolled up sandpaper (try coarse or medium grit). You can also try wrapping sandpaper around a length of dowel. A ³⁄₄" diameter dowel piece should be about the right size. In addition, a round saw rasp or a small- to medium-sized half-round rasp can also be used. *(See Figure 61.)*

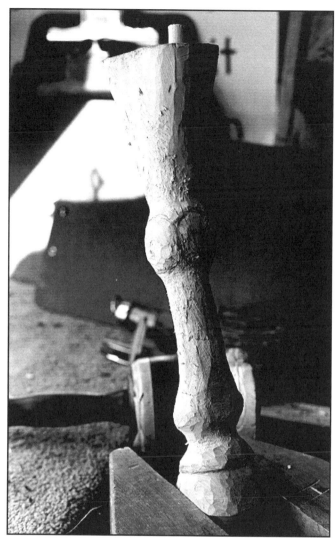

FIGURE 59 — *To carve the knobs of the knees and the fetlocks, draw circles on the wood as guides. Redraw the circles as they are carved away. The goal at this point is to remove just enough wood to suggest the shapes of the knees and the fetlocks.*

The shallow grooves in the back of the leg, which are below the knee on each side of the tendon, are somewhat short in length, as is the tendon itself. *(See Figure 62.)* At the top of these grooves, there is a gradual tapering off into the knee joint. At the bottom they trail off, on each side, into the fetlock. Don't carve straight through the fetlock at the back; just ease into it and taper off. The fetlock is tricky, as is the rest of the lower leg area. The best way to understand what the legs are all about is to observe them firsthand, if possible. Look closely at carousel horses, real horses, statues of horses and good horse models to get a good idea of the nuances around the bottom part of the legs.

To get started carving the tendon, draw two parallel lines approximately ³⁄₄" apart from a point just below the back of the knee down to

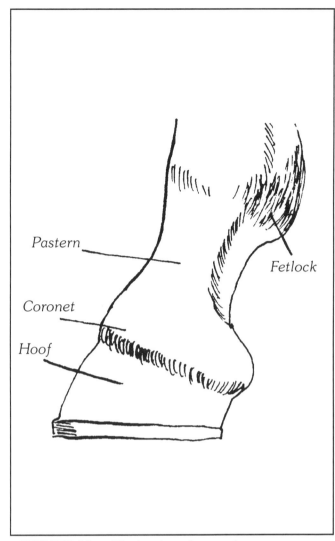

FIGURE 60 — *The hoof can be a tricky area to carve. The fetlock balloons out then curves in at the pastern. The coronet flares out just below the pastern and overhangs the hoof.*

where the fetlock begins to flare outward. These lines separate the tendon from the shallow grooves you'll be carving on either side.

You can gouge out these shallow grooves with a medium gouge. *(See Figure 63.)* Try a #6 (25mm) or #5 (20mm), if you have one of these two among your tools. Sandpaper can also be a big help as you work around the tendon and, in fact, the whole leg when used in conjunction with other tools. An excellent tool to use for more fine shaping and trimming of the leg is a spoke-shave. *(See Figure 64.)* Also, be sure to keep your chip carving knife and a riffler or two close by.

When you're ready to work around the hoof, grab a pencil. Draw a line around the hoof just below what will become the coronet, the crown-like shape above the hoof mentioned earlier. This wrap-around line will represent the top edge of the hoof. It starts low from the side of the hoof near the back, slants upward, goes around the front of the hoof, then slants downward on the other side.

Make a stop cut with your chip carving knife along the pencil line. Trim away some wood from the hoof up to the stop cut all the way around the line of the hoof. Use a riffler to accent the hoof line. This will leave a clear division between the hoof and the coronet. *(See Figures 65-1, 65-2 and 65-3.)*

A horseshoe can be indicated on the outside of each hoof by drawing a line all the way around the bottom quarter inch of the hoof. Score the line, then remove a sliver of wood from the line. Define the line with a

FIGURE 61 — *To keep the pastern from getting too thin, use a piece of rolled-up sandpaper, either coarse or medium grit, or a small to medium half-round rasp.*

riffler or with sandpaper. This narrow groove will give the illusion that there's a horseshoe on the hoof.

If you want to carve a horseshoe on the bottom of the *raised* hoof, draw a curved line on the flat part of the hoof about $^5/_{16}$" inside the edge of the wood. *(See Figures 66-1, 66-2 and 66-3.)* Follow the curvature of the hoof. It should curve in slightly toward the back on each side. Score the curved line, then make a stop cut with a V-parting tool or with your chip carving knife. Remove a thin layer of wood from inside the horseshoe with a small or medium shallow gouge. Use a riffler and #80 grit sandpaper to clean up the surface. You can carve out a V-shaped wedge from the back of the hoof to give it a more authentic appearance. This V-shape, or "frog" as it's called, is carved wide and shallow on some horses and on others it's carved as a narrow crevice, slightly puckered around the edges. Try to look at the hooves on different carousel horses, if at all possible, before deciding. One version is shown in *Figure 67*.

There's no need to carve out horseshoes on the bottom of the other three legs, since they'll be resting on a base or other surface. However, if you feel an overpowering eccentric urge to carve out the other three horseshoes, follow the same procedures as those described for the single horseshoe on the raised hoof.

The thing to remember about legs, at least carousel horse legs, is not to get carried away with them. Don't overcarve in the early stages. It's unlikely this will happen since most people approach the carving of the legs with awe, fascination and terror, not always in that order. Often, even when the horse is nearing completion, each leg resembles a knobby, lethal club. Never mind about that, you're still better off shaping the legs

slowly and cautiously. It's better to undercarve and realize you still have a ways to go, than to take off too much and have no recourse except to start a new leg.

ROUGH-SHAPING THE BACK LEGS

The most obvious difference between the back legs of a horse and the front legs is that the respective pairs bend in opposite directions; obvious to most but not to all. (There are some other differences, but they're less dramatically apparent.) Because of these structural differences, the back legs require a few additional carving instructions, over and above what's been described for the front

FIGURE 62 — *The shallow grooves in the back of the leg are short in length and taper gradually into the knee joint.*

legs. Certain areas of the legs are fairly similar—for example, the cannons, fetlocks, pasterns, coronets and hooves—so the carving these will be practically the same. Before you begin carving, be sure to mark "R" and "L" on the top or bottom of the right and left legs. *(See Figure 68.)*

At a glance, the tendon and, farther up, the hamstring seem to run without interruption almost the entire length of the back of the leg. Near the top of the leg, the hamstring tapers off into the hindquarters. At the bottom of the leg, the tendon tapers off into the fetlock. At the midway point there's a bony-looking joint called the hock, or heel bone. This joint can be emphasized in detail or merely suggested. On a horse the size of the one you're carving, it's not essential that you make intricate details in the hock area. Some of the photographs in the "Photo Gallery" show detailed examples of the back of the legs. Also, see the examples in the

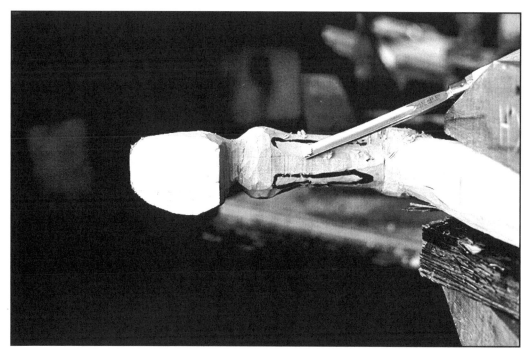

FIGURE 63 — *Use a medium gouge and sandpaper to shape the shallow area in the back of the leg.*

FIGURE 64 — *A spoke shave can be used for fine details.*

miscellaneous photographs of the legs in various stages at the end of this chapter.

Begin by carving off the sharp corners up and down the leg, following the same general carving procedures as you did on the front legs. Then, draw circles on each side of where the respective knobs of the hock and fetlocks will soon be protruding. *(See Figures 69 and 70.)* As you're carving and the circles disappear, redraw them until the knobs actually

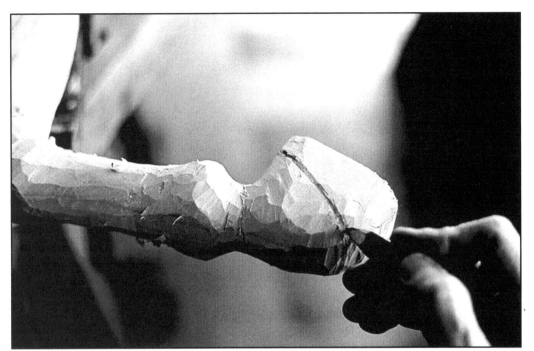

FIGURE 65-1 — *Using a pencil, draw a line just below the coronet. This line represents the top of the hoof.*

FIGURE 65-2 — *Make a stop cut with a chip carving knife along the hoof line. Remove a small amount of wood below the stop cut.*

begin to emerge from the wood as a result of your removing the surrounding wood.

Start work on the tendon by drawing two lines down the middle of the back of the leg with a ¾" width between the lines, or close to that width. Next, begin hollowing out a groove on each side of the lines with a medium shallow gouge. (Don't hesitate to draw on any lines that will help

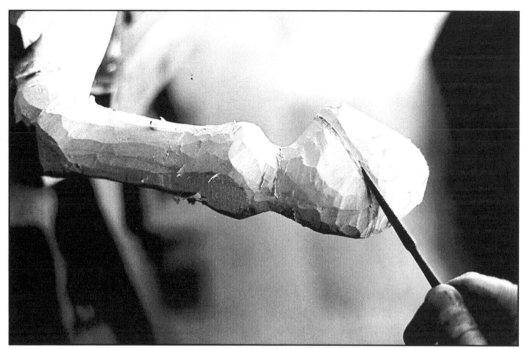

FIGURE 65-3 — Accent the hoof line with a riffler.

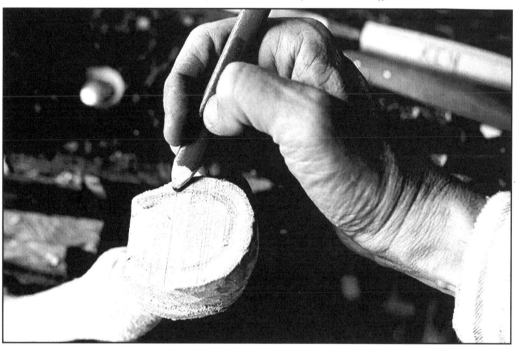

FIGURE 66-1 — To create a horseshoe on the bottom of the raised hoof, draw a line around the flat part of the hoof, 5/16" in from the edge.

guide you as you carve.) The pencil lines that run the length of the back of the leg should be redrawn after the rough-shaping, but draw them slightly closer together. They'll help later when you begin to make refinements, as things really start to shape up. *(See Figures 71-1, 71-2 and 71-3.)*

From time to time, as you carve, hold the legs in place against the respective upper leg sections on the body. This is to make sure you're not carving off too much on one side or the other. Naturally, you're not going

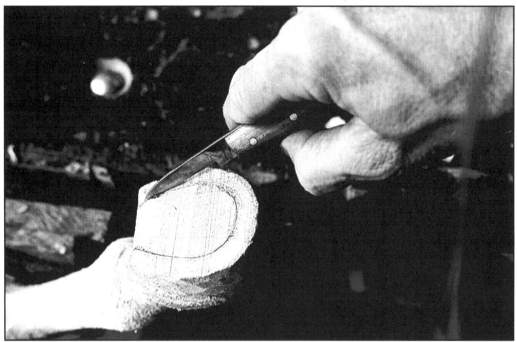

FIGURE 66-2 — *Score the line with the tip of a chip carving knife and remove a sliver of wood just to the inside of the line.*

FIGURE 66-3 — *Carve away a thin layer of wood from the inside of the hoof with a small or medium shallow gouge. Clean up the surface with a riffler or sandpaper.*

to have a perfect match-up at this stage; just see that you're not overcarving. When you've carved each of the legs into a roughly shaped facsimile of a leg, put them aside. It's time to continue working on the body. *(See Figures 72-1, 72-2.)*

Note: *Although you have a limited amount of material to carve with there's enough for you to be able to suggest a few muscles, hol-*

FIGURE 67 — *The addition of a v-shaped wedge in the back of the hoof, called a frog, gives the raised hoof a more authentic look. Frogs can be many different shapes, from wide and shallow to narrow and puckered.*

FIGURE 68 — *Labeling the legs with "L" or "R" to indicate left and right will help to avoid confusion as the horse is assembled.*

FIGURE 69 — *To shape the back leg, remove the sharp corners up and down the leg. Draw circles on each side to mark the position of the fetlock.*

FIGURE 70 — *Remove wood around the circle that marks the fetlock until the fetlock is raised above the rest of the leg.*

lows and other configurations here and there. The extent to which you eventually carve such details is a personal choice.

MISCELLANEOUS PHOTOGRAPHS - LEGS

Figures 73-1, 73-2, 73-3, 73-4, 73-5, 73-6 and 73-7 represent the legs

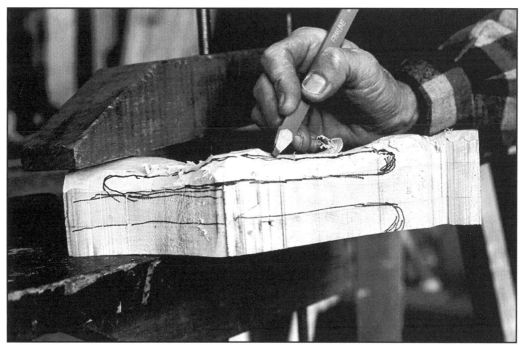

FIGURE 71-1 — *Draw guidelines for the tendons onto the back leg. The lines should be ¾" apart.*

FIGURE 71-2 — *Using a medium shallow gouge, hollow out a groove on each side of the pencil marks. Redraw the lines as needed.*

in various carving stages. They're not the last word in how the legs should be carved, only interpretations for this particular horse. But they may provide some help to you. Also, refer to the "Photo Gallery" shots and notice the different carving styles on the legs.

The hock area, which is normally carved with more intricate details on the back legs of larger horses, has been purposely simplified on this

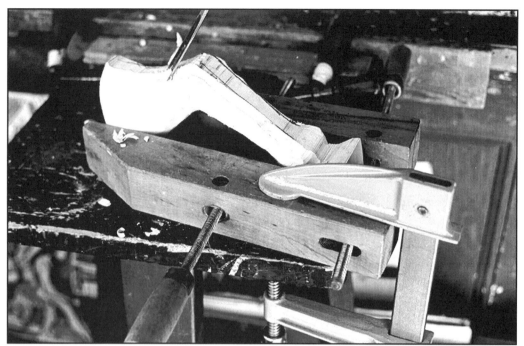

FIGURE 71-3 — *A vise will help to hold the leg securely in place and allow the use of both hands while carving.*

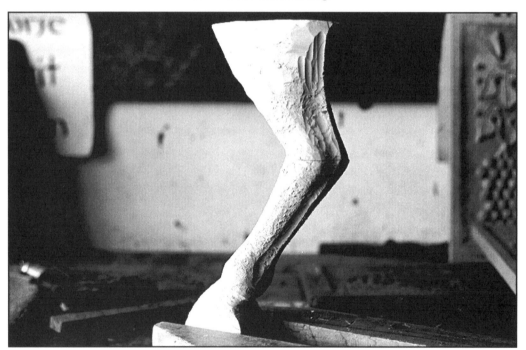

FIGURE 72-1 — *Take time out from carving to remove the leg from the vise and check your progress.*

smaller horse. If you're an advanced carver, however, you can choose to include more details after making closer observations of various carousel horses.

FIGURE 72-2 — *When both legs are similarly rough-shaped, put them aside and continue working on the body.*

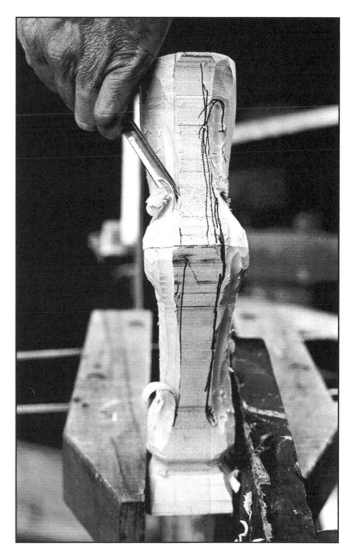

FIGURES 73-1 THROUGH 73-7 — *The following photos show legs in various stages of carving. Use them for reference as you carve the legs of your carousel horse.*

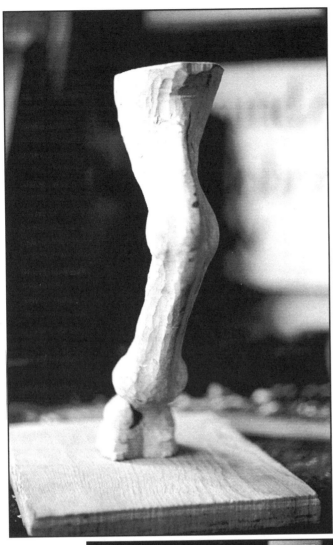

FIGURE 73-2

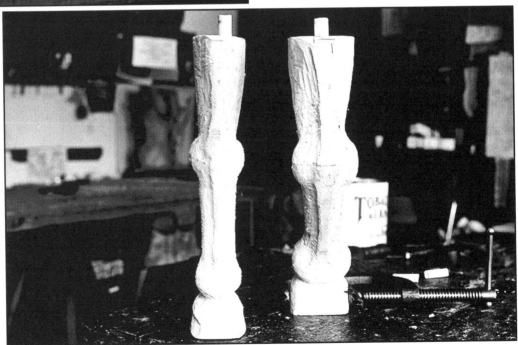

FIGURE 73-3

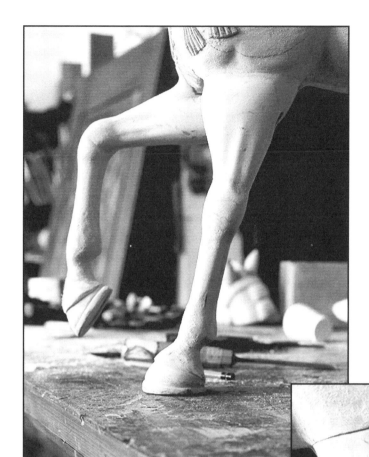

FIGURE 73-4

FIGURE 73-5

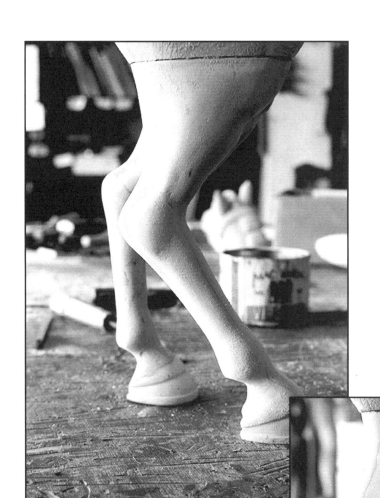

FIGURE 73-6

FIGURE 73-7

♞ *CHAPTER IV* ♞

THINKING AHEAD

Before you resume work on the body, start thinking about designs for the saddle, blanket and trappings. Trappings are straps, as well as frills and ornaments, that can be carved in relief on the horse. It may seem premature, but when you're going to include relief carving on a carousel horse you need to plan ahead. At some point during the rough-shaping stage take time out to draw your ideas on paper. Determine which trappings and miscellaneous ornaments, if any, will be in highest relief. Most likely the highest part of the relief carving on the body will be the saddle, so that's what you'll need to establish first when you begin carving out your designs. The blanket, straps and cinch belt (the girth strap under the belly to hold the saddle on) will all be carved in varying degrees of relief. The key to relief carving is using foresight regarding priorities: highest relief first, next highest after that, and so on.

In relief carving, the element of illusion is considerable and *ever* present. What this means is that the observer often sees more than is actually there, more depth, more dimension. Naturally, a less ornate design, that is to say basic with a minimum of adornment, will be less difficult to carve and sand than will a design that is elaborate in details. Regardless, the illusion will be effective.

BACK TO BODY WORK

The point of the rump gets a pretty good rounding on each side beginning approximately 3" in back of the saddle, down to where the upper leg sections begin. The area immediately behind the saddle on each side also gets rounded off, but it's more of a squared-off roundness, like a rounded corner.

As far as the neck goes, for now take off only enough to round the sharp corners, especially in back of the neck. (But don't get involved in shaping the neck, that will come later.) Also, take a little off from the corners on the front part of the neck. And if you haven't begun rounding off the corners on each side of the front of the chest, do so now. The corners are neither radically rounded nor sharply squared, but somewhere

FIGURE 74 — *Use a wide variety of woodcarving tools and a rasp to round the belly of the horse. Make sure the belly is well-rounded before beginning to add designs.*

in between. Don't rush to complete the shaping of the chest. It will evolve as you go along.

The sides of the belly should be rounded only slightly at first, because you're going to have a saddle, blanket and who knows what other bells and whistles in carved relief on both sides of the horse. Start at the midway point and gradually taper down the belly in opposite directions toward the

FIGURE 75 — *Round the bottom of the belly, cleaning up the tool marks with a flat saw rasp or a metal rasp.*

upper front and upper back leg sections. The goal is to round off the belly as well as carve out two shallow creases, or depressions, where the belly joins the legs. These creases should be slight until you get a perspective on the overall rounding process needed for the belly, including work on the saddle which will be coming up soon. Alternately use a rasp along with your woodcarving tools to arrive at a satisfactory roundness before you get involved with the designs. *(See Figure 74.)*

The bottom of the belly should not be left mostly flat with rounded corners on the sides. *(See Figure 75.)* Instead, round off the bottom as best you can. You'll have to wing it because of the potential variables concerning relief carving. Use a flat saw rasp or metal rasp to clean up the surface. Rounding the belly will probably cause you to think about the thickness of the body, if you haven't already, and whether or not you want to leave it as it is or carve it thinner. Essentially, you should let things develop in relation to the carving as a whole. Relationships will change as the carving progresses.

Go back over the areas you started on earlier, but this time begin to think more "sculpturally" as you carve. Look at the photos, look at any horse models you may have as visual aids and look at carousel horses on display or at amusement parks. Develop a selective eye for the nuances and refinements. Transfer what you see to the carving to create your own interpretation of your observations.

SAWING OUT THE RUMP

In order to make a division in the rump, you'll need a hand-held saw. *(See*

FIGURE 76 — *To make the division in the rump, use a small hand-held saw and work with the body clamped tightly to the work bench.*

Figure 76.) A small hand-held saw is best for maneuvering at an angle on each side of the rump, but if you don't have one, an ordinary household saw of standard length will do.

Measure down approximately 2" below the point on the hind quarters where the tail will eventually be plugged in. Make a pencil mark at this point. Turn the body upside down and draw a line beginning from the mark you just made, then along the center of the rear end to a point about midway inside the upper legs. Use common sense in determining the length of the line. There's no need to try and gut the horse. About 2" on the underside should do it.

Begin by sawing down along the center line. Don't saw too deeply. Ease up at each end of the line. The saw cut should be made in such a way that it follows an imaginary convex curve between the legs. Then, saw inward at an angle from the outer part of the center line on one side. Stop sawing when the blade meets the center line saw cut and the wedge of wood begins to give way. *(See Figure 77.)* Remove the wedge of wood. (And no jokes, just throw it away.) Repeat this procedure on the other side of the cut.

The rump can be shaped with gouges, rasps, rifflers and coarse and medium sandpaper. For now, however, a little cleaning up of the surface is all that's needed. *(See Figure 78.)*

As long as you're working around the underside, place the legs flush against the respective upper leg sections on the body. Draw a line around the top part of each leg. *(See Figure 79.)* The

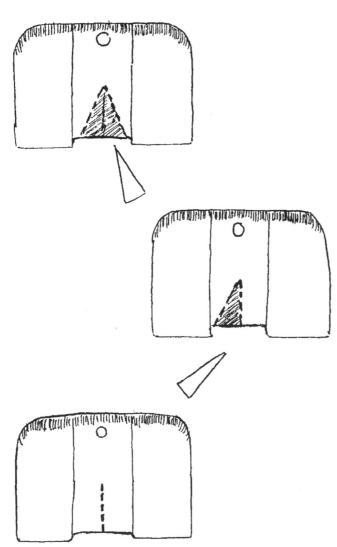

FIGURE 77 — *Saw along a center line following the imaginary convex curve between the legs. Then saw inward at an angle. Stop when the blade meets the center cut. Do the same on the opposite side of the first saw cut.*

♞ Carousel Horse Carving ♞

oval markings you draw will let you know how far you should carve without straying into the area where the legs will be attached to the body. These markings are not finite, since you're still honing everything down. They're just temporary guides as you make your way along.

While the body is upside down, attend to the short span of wood that bridges the back legs, where you sawed out the rump, as well as the wood between the front legs. If you want to knock out some of the excess wood in these areas, carve out a shallow groove between the legs using a large gouge. (See Figures 80 and 81.) A rasp or medium riffler with a curved head

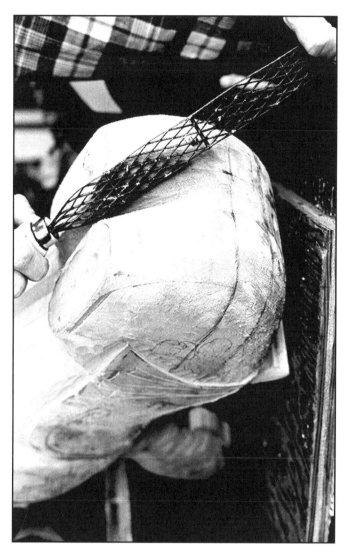

FIGURE 78 — Shape the rump with gouges, rasps, rifflers and sandpaper.

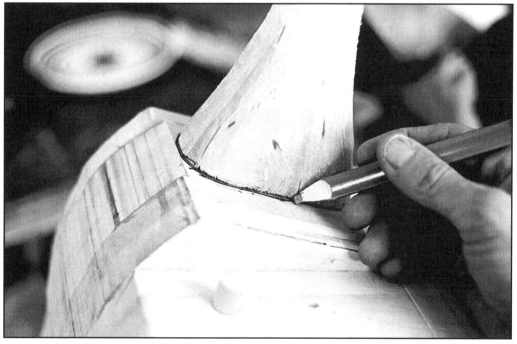

FIGURE 79 — Place the legs against the underside of the body and trace around them with a pencil. These lines will act as guidelines to show how much wood to remove from the body.

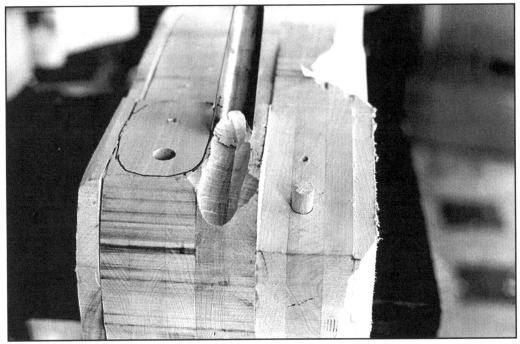

FIGURE 80 — *Carve a shallow groove in the body between the rear legs with a large gouge.*

FIGURE 81 — *Additional shaping can be done with smaller gouges, a rasp or a medium riffler with a curved head on one end.*

on at least one end can be used for additional shaping and for any cleaning up.

CHEST MUSCLES

The prominent muscles on a horse's chest resemble two bulging ovoid-like shapes and cover a good portion of the lower front chest. Between and below these muscles is a pronounced cleavage, or cleft. Because the chest is end grain, it's not an eagerly awaited area of the body to work on. Fortunately, you'll be carving out trappings which means you can get away with making what could be referred to as "peek-a-boo" chest muscles above and below the strap or straps. In fact, with an elaborate chest strap design you can avoid carving any more than the barest suggestion of chest muscles, unless it's something you strongly want to see on the horse. Minimizing the chest muscles depends on how much clutter (strap width, more than one strap and tassels) you can come up with to cover the chest.

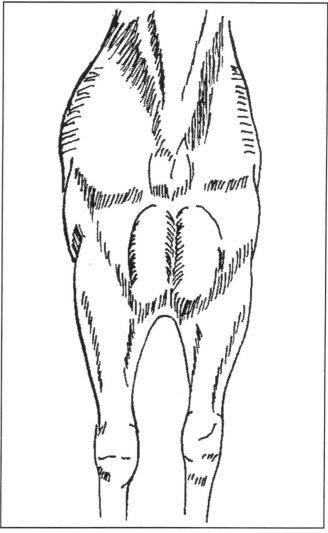

FIGURE 82 — *The suggestion of chest muscles is often overlooked on carousel horses. You may opt to carve lines for the chest muscles or omit them.*

The lower part of the cleavage is the area between the upper front legs where they join the chest. *(See Figure 82.)* Although this muscle division is often pronounced on real horses, it's not always carved with great emphasis on carousel horses. Sometimes this area is simply rounded off with only a slight crease carved or filed out to suggest the cleavage. Occasionally, it's completely ignored. The better carvers usually incorporated chest muscles into the overall carving. It's a decision you'll have to make for yourself. Don't let it hold you up; it's not a crucial part of the whole carving.

There are related muscles around the chest and shoulder areas that are part of a complex of muscles. Although these muscles are important, it's not going to make a substantial difference if they are not carved in detail on your scaled-down horse. If you do want to include such details, study the chest and shoulder muscles on standard-sized carousel horses shown in the "Photo Gallery" and in books on horses and carousels.

DESIGNING THE SADDLE, BLANKET AND TRAPPINGS

Deciding what to do about a saddle, blanket and trappings can be an exasperating experience. Which designs do you choose when you have such a bountiful variety of styles to consider? Try studying the various styles and let yourself focus in on the designs that your eye keeps going back to. Use the process of elimination until you're down to a few choices. Then, let practical considerations make your decision. If a particular design you favor is so elaborate that it's unlikely anyone but a master woodcarver could pull it off, go with the less complicated design— unless, of course, you are a master woodcarver. In one sense, it's admirable for someone to come up with an ambitious, intricate set of designs, but it's most important to keep in mind one's level of experience in carving relief on a three-dimensional object.

One method of copying a design is to use a slide projector. First, get a large sheet of blank paper. Outline the profile of the horse you're carving on the paper as best you can. Tape the sheet of paper onto a wall or door. Then, project a slide of the carousel horse you've selected to use for trappings and other design purposes onto the sheet of paper. Adjust the size of the slide by moving the projector forward or backward. With the projector running, go up to the sheet of paper and trace over the superimposed designs.

Another way to come up with designs is to copy the outline of the horse pattern shown in the pattern section of this book. Make several photocopies or carbon copies, then fill in the blanks. In other words, make up your own designs or a composite based on designs from different styles and draw them onto the copies of the horse to see what appeals to you. Later, you can color them in with crayons or colored pencils to arrive at a color scheme. A composite can bring a sense of uniqueness and individual personality to the horse.

Whichever designs you choose and however you go about applying them to the wood, even if temporary, make sure you do it before going much further with the horse. It's essential that you have a clear idea, at this stage, of what you will be carving in relief on the body.

TRANSFERRING THE DESIGNS TO THE HORSE

Once you've decided on the designs to be carved on the body, you'll need to get them onto the wood. Here are a few suggestions, one of which you might find useful.

Place the body on its side on a piece of plain wrapping paper or other large scrap paper. Draw the outline of the horse onto the paper. If you used the slide projector idea, you don't need to make another outline of the body to copy out designs, unless you'd like to have a spare or two. Now begin experimenting with your ideas by penciling in the designs. When you're satisfied cut out the designs. You can use these paper designs as crude templates to tape onto the body. Then, draw around the design outlines directly onto the wood.

An alternative to cutting out the designs from paper is to place a transparent sheet of "prepared" acetate over the drawings on the paper. ("Prepared" is a type of acetate sheet to which a felt tip pen can be applied.) Then, copy the designs onto the acetate sheet with a felt tip pen. Next, cut out the designs from the acetate sheet. Tape these acetate templates to the body and trace around the outline. The straps going around the rump and chest can be joined together on the wood after the designs have been drawn on both sides of the body.

The reason for suggesting an acetate sheet is that you might find this flexible material easier and more durable to work with than paper. Most of the larger art supply stores carry prepared acetate sheets, as well as felt tip pens. Many plastics outlets also carry acetate. Another advantage in using a clear acetate sheet as a template of sorts is that you can see through it to more accurately line up of the designs. Any details within the outline designs can be transferred a couple of ways.

One way to negotiate the transfer is to tape the top part of the cut-out template to the body. Then, lift the bottom half of the acetate template and draw the details onto the wood as best you can, eyeballing the designs. A more reliable way is to tape graphite paper, available in art supply stores, to the areas where the designs are to be transferred. When the templates are taped over the graphite paper, draw over the felt tip drawn designs with a pencil, exerting extra pressure as you go. This procedure will leave a dark, semi-smudged impression of the design on the wood. When the acetate templates and graphite papers are removed, you can draw over the designs to make the markings more clear.

If you have an artistic touch you may want to draw the designs directly onto the wood free-hand. Actually, if you plan to use relatively basic designs, you don't need to be artistic to draw them on the wood. Basic designs usually amount to simple geometry. For instance, straps that wrap around the rump or slant down the shoulders and go across the chest can be marked on the wood with a pencil and a flexible ruler. Make sure the marks line up on both sides of the horse. You can always erase or sand off any mistakes.

Although a felt tip pen has been mentioned as a drawing implement to use when making pattern outlines, *do not* use one for making marks or transferring designs directly onto the wood. It could bleed through and cause problems during the refining and finishing stages. A thick, dark pencil, available at most hardware or art supply stores, is the best type of marker to use.

If you're going to draw the saddle and blanket designs on the wood free-hand, here's a way to transfer the designs to the other side for a balanced match-up. After you've drawn the designs on one side, tape a piece of tracing paper over it. You might have to cut into the tracing paper to make it lie firmly against the curve of the top of the saddle. Then, with a marking pencil, draw over the designs on the wood so that they're transferred to the tracing paper. Remove the tracing paper and turn it over. Draw over the design showing through on the back of the tracing paper.

Next, tape a piece of carbon paper onto the unmarked side of the body. Be sure you test the carbon paper to see that the correct side is against the wood. Tape the tracing paper over the carbon paper so that the reverse side of the designs are facing outward. After you line up the designs correctly, draw over them so that they are transferred to the body. When the tracing and carbon papers are removed, you'll have enough of an idea of the designs to retrace them with your pencil. If you discover that somehow you've misaligned the designs on the wood, sand or file them off and try it again. Always keep a copy or rough drawing of the designs, just in case part of the lines get rubbed off or carved off.

INITIAL CARVING OF THE SADDLE, BLANKET AND TRAPPINGS

Score the saddle, blanket and trapping lines with a chip carving knife or a V-parting tool. (It isn't absolutely necessary that you begin on the trappings now, they can wait. The most important objective at this point

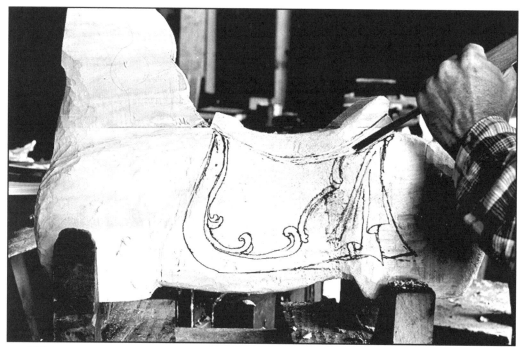

FIGURE 83-1 — *Draw the saddle blanket and trapping lines with a pencil and score them with a carving knife or v-parting tool.*

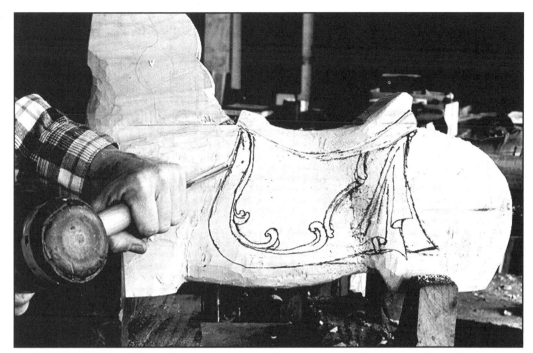

FIGURE 83-2 — Trim off just enough wood to suggest the beginning of relief carving. More wood will be removed later.

is to establish the saddle and a blanket or blankets.) In any case, begin trimming off wood just to the outside of these cuts. Take off only enough to suggest the beginning of relief carving. Do not get involved in anything more then starting basic carving lines. *(See Figures 83-1 and 83-2.)*

FIGURE 84 — Use a medium shallow gouge and a draw knife to remove wood from the area where the pommel, the back of the shoulders and the base of the neck converge. This area is called the withers.

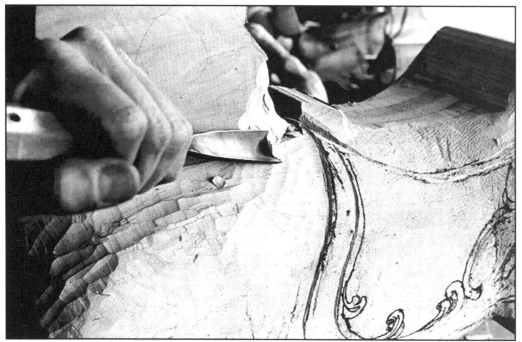

FIGURE 85-1 — *Carefully carve up to the shallow relief carving at the edge of the saddle.*

FIGURE 85-2 — *Keep several different sizes of gouges handy as you work this area and ease up on the tool as you come close to the saddle.*

At the front of the saddle, start to carve up and in toward the pommel using a medium shallow gouge. Try to control the carving so that you take off the wood with finer shaving strokes. A draw knife can also be used to help remove wood and begin the shaping of this area. Most likely you'll need to re-establish at least part of the saddle design near the pommel as you continue to make this area more narrow at the top. It seems to be unavoidable when the front of the saddle is being shaped. *(See Figure 84.)* The area where the pommel, the back of the shoulders and the base of the neck, at the back, all converge is referred to as the "withers;" a very tricky place to shape.

In order to get at this area, you'll have to carve off some wood at the back of the neck on each side. Take off only enough so that you can maneuver around at the back of the shoulders near the forward part of the saddle. As you carve up to the shallow relief you started at the front of the saddle, ease up with the carving tool that you're using to avoid carving through the relief. Keep a few different gouges close by and experiment with them. *(See Figures 85-1 and 85-2.)*

Lengthwise, there's a very shallow curvature to the seat of the saddle along the top. It would be best to use a rasp or other filing tool to slightly round off the top of the seat to minimize the removal of surface wood. Whatever you do, try not to let the profile line along the seat dip much below the profile line of the back of the horse behind the saddle; otherwise, the credibility of the horse's profile will be at stake. Keep in mind that the saddle is supposed to be resting on the horse's back.

There should be an emphatic roundness across the *width* of the saddle. *(See Figure 86.)* While you work on the saddle, think about a little rider having to sit on the seat you're shaping. Make it as comfortable and as natural a fit as possible.

Now that the saddle, blanket and, possibly, some of the trappings have been started, you can either continue carving if you want to give more depth to the relief areas, or leave them for now and begin shaping the neck.

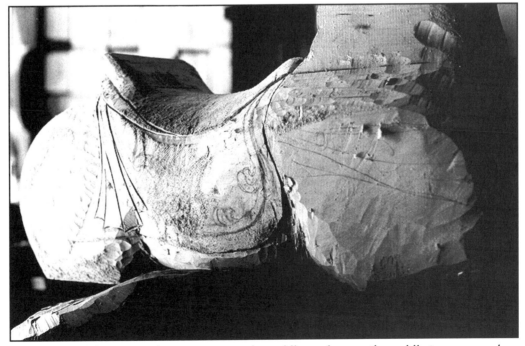

FIGURE 86 — *As work progresses on the saddle, make sure the saddle is very round. Keep the small rider who will be sitting in the saddle in mind as you carve.*

FIGURE 87-1 — *Temporarily attach the head to the neck.*

Approach the carving of the neck as you did the body. That is to say, rather than spending a lot of time carving on one side before moving on to the other side, work the neck as a whole within the limits described on the next few pages. As you begin to work on the neck, think about what type of mane you'd like to carve. The mane will be discussed later, after you've begun to shape the neck.

Before you secure the body, a few marks can be drawn on the neck to be used as guidelines until you get further along. First, draw a wide oval on the flat surface where the head will be attached later. *(See Figures 87-1 and 87-2.)* The size of the oval should be fairly generous to start. This mark is to help you get a sense of how far you should round off the corners, initially, as you work your way around the wood.

The top of the neck is narrow where it joins the head compared to the base where it gets thicker and flows into the body. On each side of the neck, there's a muscle that begins just below the ears and runs the length of the neck. (Because the head will not be attached while you work on the neck, this reference to ears is meaningless to you at this point. So just think of the muscle as running along the curve of the neck, at the side.)

On the right side, where the mane will eventually be carved, this long muscle will most likely be covered up by the strands.

When you start to work on the left side, use shallow gouges to taper the wood toward the back from an imaginary line running along the middle of the neck. *(See Figure 88.)*

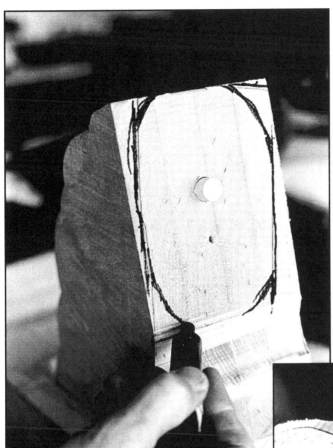

FIGURE 87-2 — Draw a large oval on the flat surface of the neck. These lines will act as a guideline for removing wood from the neck.

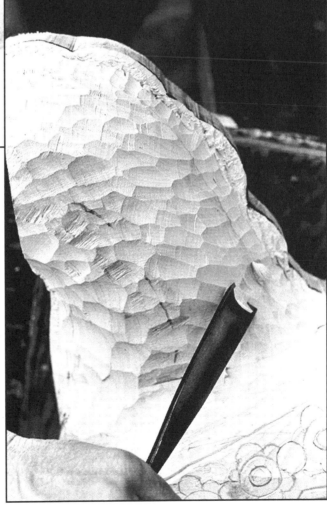

FIGURE 88 — Using a shallow gouge, remove wood from the mane. Taper the cuts toward an imaginary line that runs down the center of the mane.

FIGURE 89 — *Continue carving toward the front of the neck using the shallow gouge.*

Next, start carving over toward the front of the neck. *(See Figure 89.)* Begin shaping the slight bulge that resembles a long Adam's apple. Use rasps and rifflers. *(See Figure 90.)* On each side of this narrow, rounded area are concave hollows that run the length of the neck. They can be as deep and accented or as shallow and subtle as you want to make them. These jugular grooves, as they are called, should be carved out with a shallow gouge and with rifflers and coarse and medium sandpaper. The grooves become narrower as they travel down the neck. As they reach the base of the neck they begin to move closer together, a little like the front of your own neck. A flat saw rasp or metal rasp can be used to help shape the front of the neck after the initial carving has been done. *(See Figure 91.)*

At the base, there's a downward sloping on each side of the neck where it joins up, respectively, with the shoulders. These gentle sloping curves begin to move in toward each other in the middle. *(See Figure 92.)*

Working around the base of the front of the neck will bring your attention to the downward angle of the shoulders on each side of the body. Be sure you carve enough of a slant to the shoulders before you get too far along on the body straps, as you get back to them. When the angle has been satisfactorily established on each side of the shoulders, stand back and take a good look at what you've done so far to see that each side is even with the other.

Although the mane will be discussed in more detail later, it needs to be addressed briefly now. To begin with, in order to carve a mane, you'll need to leave an extra clump of wood on the right side of the neck. (Just keep this in mind for right now.) On the exposed left side, the top of the

FIGURE 90 — Use gouges, rasps and rifflers to begin shaping the large Adam's apple-like bulge in the horse's neck.

FIGURE 91 — A flat saw rasp or metal rasp is used to shape the front of the neck after the original shaping has been done.

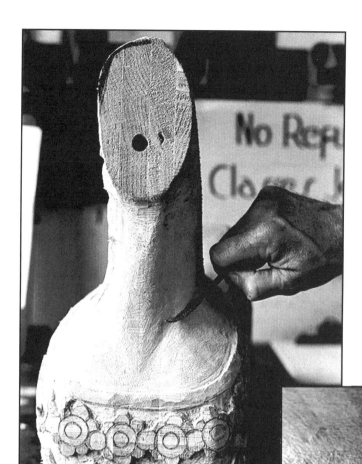

FIGURE 92 — *Carve the downward slope of the shoulders on each side of the neck. Be sure that both sides are even before you proceed.*

FIGURE 93 — *To create the mane, remove enough wood from each side of the neck so that the wood for the mane stands out about ¾" along the back of the neck.*

Alertly perked ears and wide open eyes give this Herschell-Spillman an innocent expression. (Herschell-Spillman)

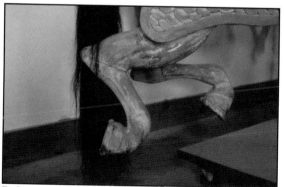

Bulging muscles and tightly tucked legs give this Stein & Goldstein jumper a powerful masculine look. (Stein & Goldstein)

The mane of this Carmel stander has a beautiful, natural rhythm to it that is repeated in the fringe and back drape. (Carmel)

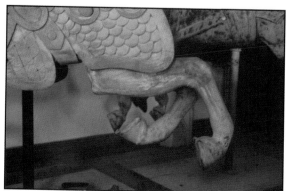

Armored horses were a favorite theme for carousel carvers in America; the overlapping disk patterns, or fish-scale armor, would protect the horse and knight in real battles. (Stein & Goldstein)

The grace and action in this pose come from the tension in the neck and the windblown flowing mane, face outstretched, leg lifted and tucked. (Mueller/Dentzel)

N Carousel Horse Carving N

Mane and forelock direction and line detail can add liveliness and excitement to a static pose. (Philadelphia Toboggan Company–PTC)

Varying the direction and curves of the mane segments lends a more natural appearance. (Dentzel)

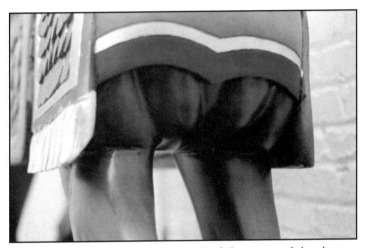

Chest trapping lines sometimes accented the curves of the chest muscles, although many have simple straight bands that were detailed with painted scrollwork instead. (Carmel)

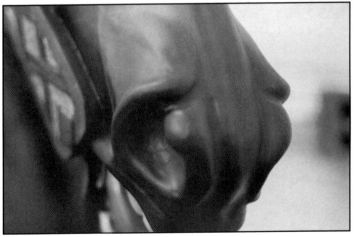

Nostrils are one of the more challenging areas of the face to carve; studying photos of real horses may help you to understand their forms. (Philadelphia Toboggan Company–PTC)

The forward sweep of this forelock, gentle eyes and less of a tuck to the head soften this pose. (Philadelphia Toboggan Company–PTC)

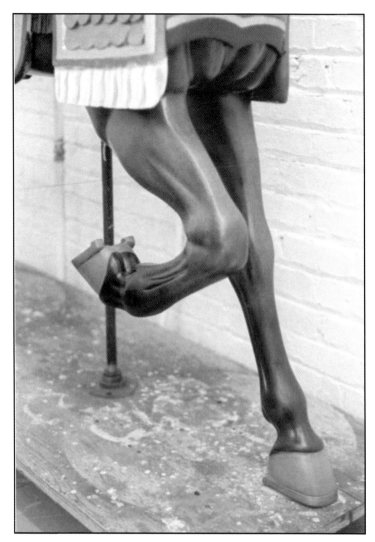

Bulging chest muscles and a high lift on the leg give this horse a restrained yet active pose. (Carmel)

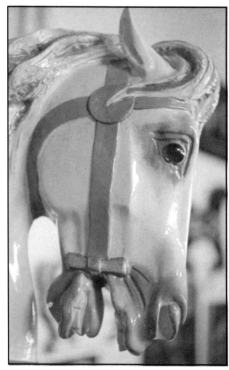

The backswept forelock, back-turned ears, tucked head and wide-open eyes give this horse an expression of wariness or fear. (Philadelphia Toboggan Company–PTC)

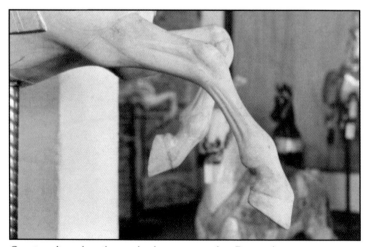

Carving fine details on the legs, as on this Dentzel, requires patience, sharp tools and some knowledge of equine anatomy. (Dentzel)

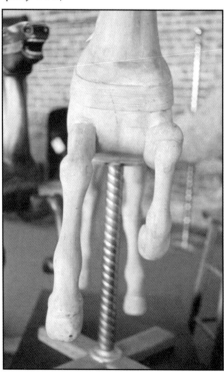

This Dentzel prancer has minimal muscle tone on the chest, focusing attention on the rear legs that support it. (Dentzel)

🐎 **Carousel Horse Carving** 🐎

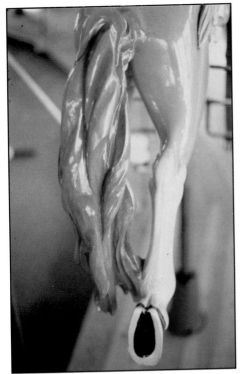

The carver of this horse utilized the fetlock as an anchor point for securing the tail. (Philadelphia Toboggan Company–PTC)

A carousel, with its infinite variety of poses and textures and movement and sound, is an invitation to a world of enchantment. (Herschell-Spillman)

Big kids and little kids alike clamor for more since one ride is never enough. (Herschell-Spillman)

The tilt of the head and flared nostrils create a lively, spirited look on this jumper. (Mueller)

Simple trappings can be enlivened with paint. (Herschell-Spillman)

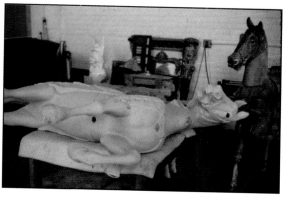

Top: The arched curve of the rear legs on this Mueller jumper are echoed in the shadow of the rear muscles as well as in the shape and curve of the trappings at the front and back. (Mueller)

Top Left: The saracen-like sword and scabbard may have been carved separately and then glued on before the horse was painted. (Herschell-Spillman)

Middle Left: The simple static poses of these carousel ponies are brought to "life" with painted patterns and detail, not jewels and glitter. (Herschell-Spillman)

Top Right: The undersides of the horses are simple and smooth with minimal detail. (Illinois)

The skull and muscle structures are well-defined by subtly carved grooves and swells. (Herschell-Spillman)

Carving veins is a more advanced technique and not all that necessary or even desirable when carving the face. (Philadelphia Toboggan Company–PTC)

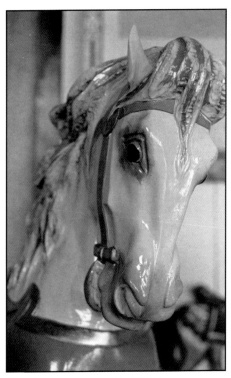

The cheek strap on this PTC horse follows the contours of the face. (Philadelphia Toboggan Company–PTC)

Notice the "frog," or groove, carved into the bottom of this Carmel hoof. (Carmel)

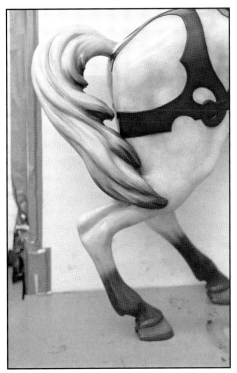

The segments of hair carved on this Dentzel's tail are simple but elegant. Note how the lines do not parallel the outside shape of the tail. (Dentzel)

After carving the romance, or right side of the mane, the opposite side without the bulk of mane is a welcome relief. (Herschell-Spillman)

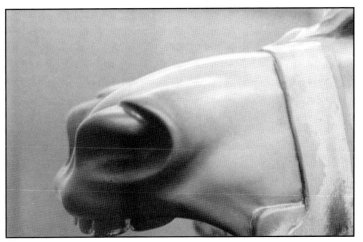

Nostrils can be a good source for depicting expression—wide, dilated ones give the horse a wild look. (Dentzel)

A long shallow groove follows the curve of the neck on each side. (Dentzel)

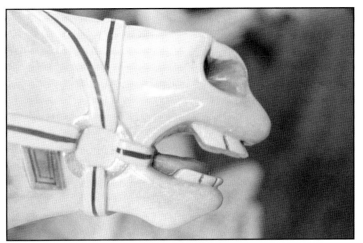

Some nostril designs, such as on this Herschell-Spillman, are simple. (Herschell-Spillman)

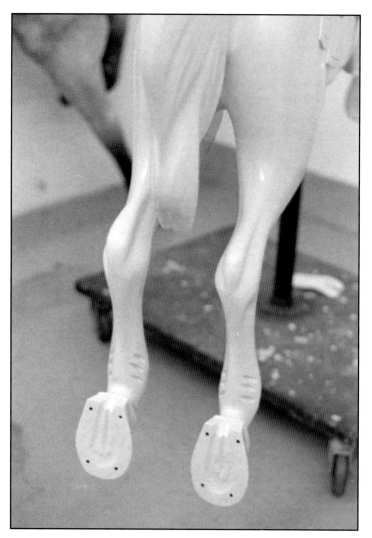

Bridle bits are quite varied; some basic research will help you decide which are appropriate for your carving projects. (Herschell-Spillman)

Spillman Engineering Company produced a less realistic, more stylized type of leg and tail. (Spillman Engineering Co.)

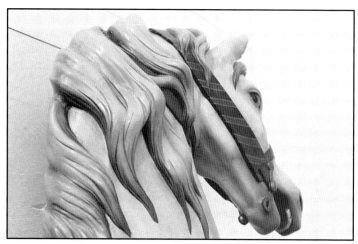

Be certain to leave enough excess wood if you plan to carve a mane with high full segments. (Dentzel)

The folds of skin carved around the eyes of this horse add a touch of realism, as does the forelock overlapping the bridle band. (Philadelphia Toboggan Company–PTC)

mane needs to be started. This is done by carving wood away from the left side at the top of the neck, slightly off-center as described in the next paragraph. The wood is carved out all the way down the back of the neck so that the mane appears to be emerging from the neck. You'll only need to leave about $3/4$" of wood standing up to get this effect. *(See Figure 93.)*

Begin by drawing a line slightly to the left of center, about $3/4$" over, along the back of the neck. Score the line all the way down, then make a stop cut with a V-parting tool. Next, take a medium shallow gouge and begin carving from the upper left side of the neck over to the stop cut. As you carve, make a new stop cut over the old one along the same path. When you've removed

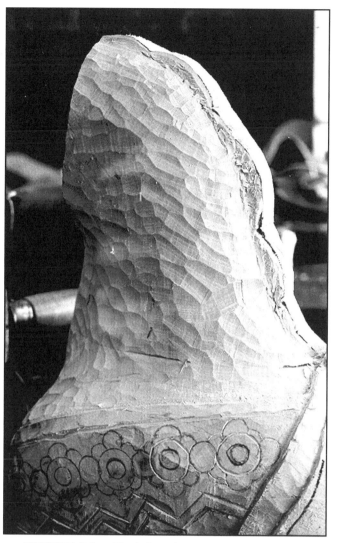

FIGURE 94 — To define the mane, score a line all the way down the mane and make a stop cut with a v-parting tool. Use a medium shallow gouge to remove wood up to the stop cut. Make another scoring cut and continue carving until the mane is clearly standing above the neck.

enough wood so that the edge of the mane is clearly standing up from the neck, clean up the surface with a riffler and move on. *(See Figure 94.)*

Move on to rounding off the top center of the mane, only slightly at first because you'll need as much surplus as possible until you refine the segments. Use a medium shallow gouge for this early stage of removing the excess wood. Clean up the surface with a saw rasp or a metal rasp. *(See Figures 95-1 and 95-2.)*

Using the design you've decided on for the mane, start outlining the segments on the wood making bold, dark pencil marks. The details (strands within each segment) will be applied later. If you're still not sure what kind of mane you want to have on your horse, try experimenting on

---

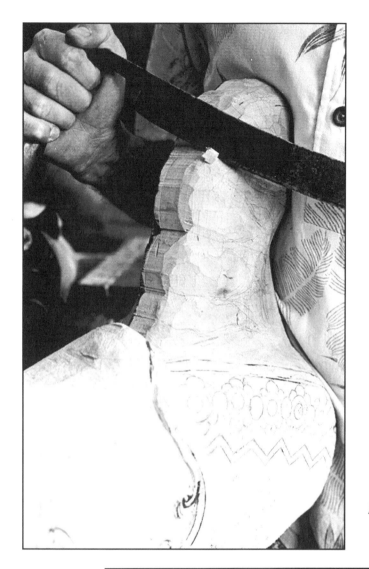

FIGURE 95-1 — Use a medium shallow gouge to round off the top center of the mane.

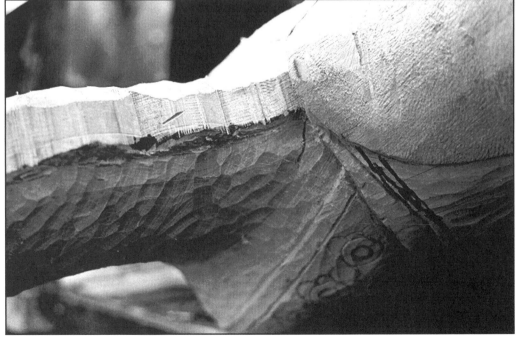

FIGURE 95-2 — Clean up the surface of the wood with a saw rasp or a metal rasp.

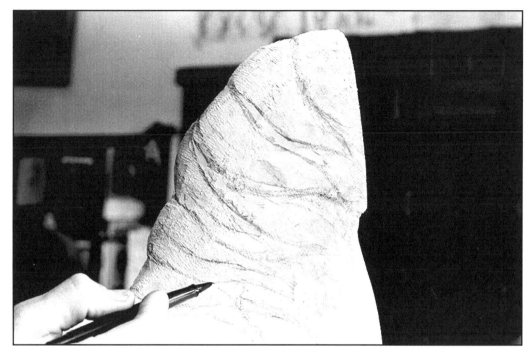

FIGURE 96 — *Outline the general shape of the various segments of the mane. Use varying lengths and overlap them occasionally.*

paper. Draw out a few different styles, trace over photographs or make use of the copy pattern in the pattern section at the end of this book.

Usually the mane consists of several segments of varying lengths, often angling across the right side of the neck at anywhere from a 30° to 45° angle. The segments are what you need to concentrate on first. The strands will come later. *(See Figure 96.)*

When you've drawn the segments on the wood, score them with your

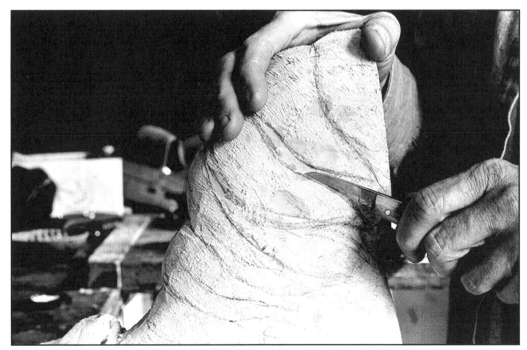

FIGURE 97-1 — *Score the lines of the mane segments with a chip carving knife.*

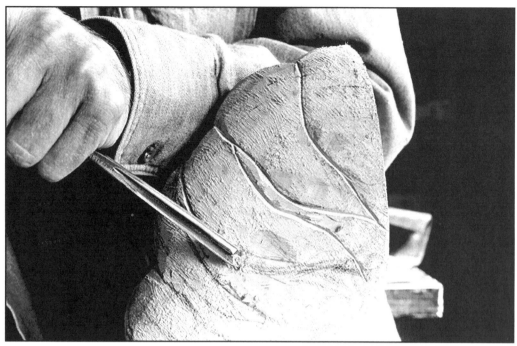

FIGURE 97-2 — Make stop cuts by following along the score lines with a v-parting tool.

chip carving knife, then follow up with a V-parting tool to make stop cuts around each segment. *(See Figures 97-1 and 97-2)*

    When the stop cuts have been made, use a shallow gouge or a chisel or skew to remove a thin layer of wood outside of and up to the border of the mane. *(See Figure 98.)* This jagged border will leave a clear separa-

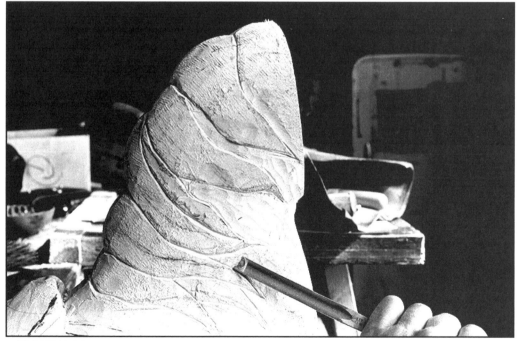

FIGURE 98 — With a shallow gouge, chisel or skew, remove a thin layer of wood along the outside of the mane. Make a clear separation between the wood of the mane and that of the neck.

tion between the mane and the neck. It will allow you to easily see what remains to be carved and shaped on the neck below the promontories and inlets of the mane.

Since the neck still needs additional shaping, don't begin carving out details on the mane yet. As you continue to shape and refine the neck, try to look at the neck of a three-dimensional horse, real or carved, to get a better sense of the contours and proportions.

CARVING THE STRANDS OF THE MANE

Decide what kind of strands you want to carve within each segment. Do you want to carve out broadly spaced strands suggesting casually arranged locks of thick hair, or do you want numerous clearly defined strands requiring more attention to detail? Study different styles of carousel horse manes before you make a decision. Notice how the carvers worked the wood so that sometimes the strands overlapped or disappeared under one another part way down or occasionally angled off in a different direction from the immediate bunch.

The best way to approach the carving is to isolate and work on one segment at a time. Be sure the surface of the wood is roughly filed or sanded off so you'll have a reasonably smooth surface to draw any guidelines on. A variety of tools can be used to carve out the strands including a chip carving knife, medium and small V-parting tools, medium and small gouges and #80 grit

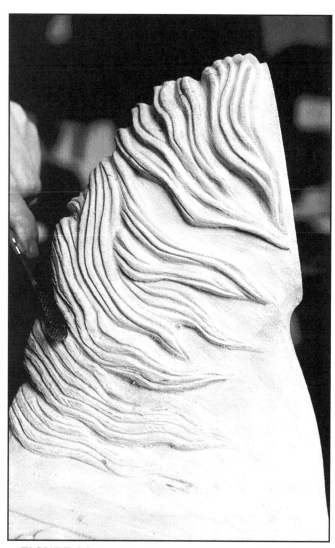

FIGURE 99-1 — *Working on one segment at a time, draw in hairs on each section of the mane. Use a variety of tools, including a chip carving knife, small and medium v-parting tools, small and medium gouges and sandpaper.*

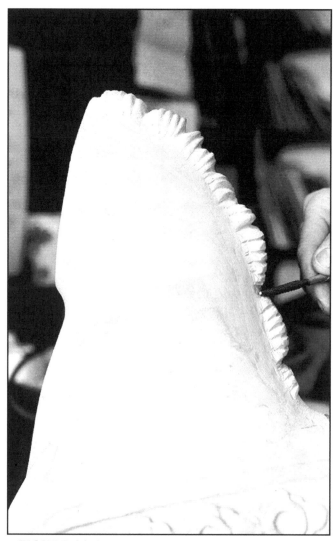

FIGURE 99-2 — *The opposite side of the neck shows only a small amount of hair. Rifflers can be used to define the strands of hair.*

sandpaper. Rifflers can also be used to advantage in helping to define the strands, regardless of the style you've decided upon. *(See Figures 99-1 and 99-2.)*

Begin by drawing lines from the top of each segment downward. No matter what style you carve, don't make straight rigid-looking strands. Give the mane a little personality. (And leave room for maneuvering the tools.) You could let a few lines go all the way down the length of the segment while others could be made shorter. Or, you could have the strands trail off or run into longer strands. There are many variations you can come up with if you put your imagination into high gear. It's up to you.

If you're making specific, detailed strands, score the lines with your chip carving knife. Make deeper grooves by following along the scored lines with a small V-parting tool. If you don't have one, use your chip carving knife to carve out a sliver of wood alongside each cut to make narrow grooves. After you've carved out the strands, go over the grooves with a riffler.

If you're making broadly shaped strands with less details, start out with a medium gouge of your choice and follow up with a few smaller gouges. Clean up the surface of the strands with sandpaper.

Each segment on the mane should have its own rhythm. Try to combine a variety of flowing movements into a harmonic arrangement. Make each segment just slightly different from the others. It will make the mane more interesting to work on and to look at when you're finished and the horse is painted.

TEMPORARILY ASSEMBLING THE BODY AND LEGS

When you've done about as much shaping on the neck and mane as you can, or should do at this stage, go back over the body again. Draw circles, lines or shadings on those places you want to shave down, scoop out, taper off and so on. This is not the final round, just the start of the refining process. After you've made some progress, put the body aside and begin fine-shaping the legs, using the same marking procedures as you did on the body. By marking the places that need to be worked on, you'll be able to immediately focus in on where you left off in case you start to work on another part (or if you have to stop for a few days because your life keeps getting in the way of the carving.)

When you begin to refine the legs, a few tools and materials that you'll find useful are as follows: a spokeshave, chip carving knife, riffler with at least one curved filing head, round file or medium half-round rasp and #80 grit sandpaper. Also, keep a medium gouge or two around in case you need to do more carving on the grooves.

After you've made further refinements, attach the legs to the body using 2" and 2½" #10 roundhead screws. This assemblage is temporary only; it's so that you can determine what adjustments have to be made in order to blend the body and legs into a cohesively shaped unit. *(See Figure 100.)*

When the horse is assembled and standing upright, make the appropriate markings on the wood; the appropriate markings being whatever you think needs to be attended to at this point. You can leave the horse as

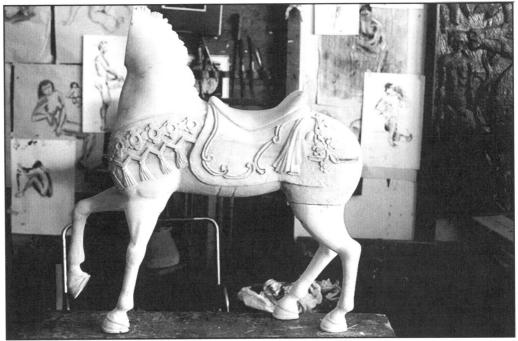

FIGURE 100 — *Check the overall progress and make any adjustments necessary at this point.*

FIGURE 101 — *Temporarily assemble the body, the legs and the neck.*

it is for awhile, intact, and work on it that way, or you can unscrew the legs from the body and start making any adjustments or refinements on the separate parts. *(See Figure 101.)* Don't be in too big of a hurry though, because the real work, the head, is next on the agenda right after a few brief words about carving the tail.

THE TAIL

Carving the tail is a matter of choosing a style, as you did with the mane, and following through with it. The strands should be of various lengths, but mostly long. *(See Figure 102.)* Consider carving the tail in such a way that the strands have some curves to them or, as a whole, start to twist slightly to the right beginning at about the midway point from top to bottom. Take a good look at what you've done so far and think about carving the tail so that it complements the style and personality of the horse. This consideration will make the tail look like an integral part of the carved horse, instead of an awkward afterthought.

Sketch out a few styles on paper. Then, when you've made a decision, draw a few strands at a time onto the wood. Carve out narrow grooves from the strand lines using your chip carving knife, a small or medium V-parting tool and several small gouges. Repeat this routine all over the tail. When the strands are carved to your satisfaction, refine the grooves with a few rifflers along with a heavy dependence on medium and fine grit sandpaper.

Another possibility for a tail is to use real horse hair in place of a carved tail. Some carousel horses sport real horse hair stuck into their rumps. If this alternative is to your liking, call up some leather retail or

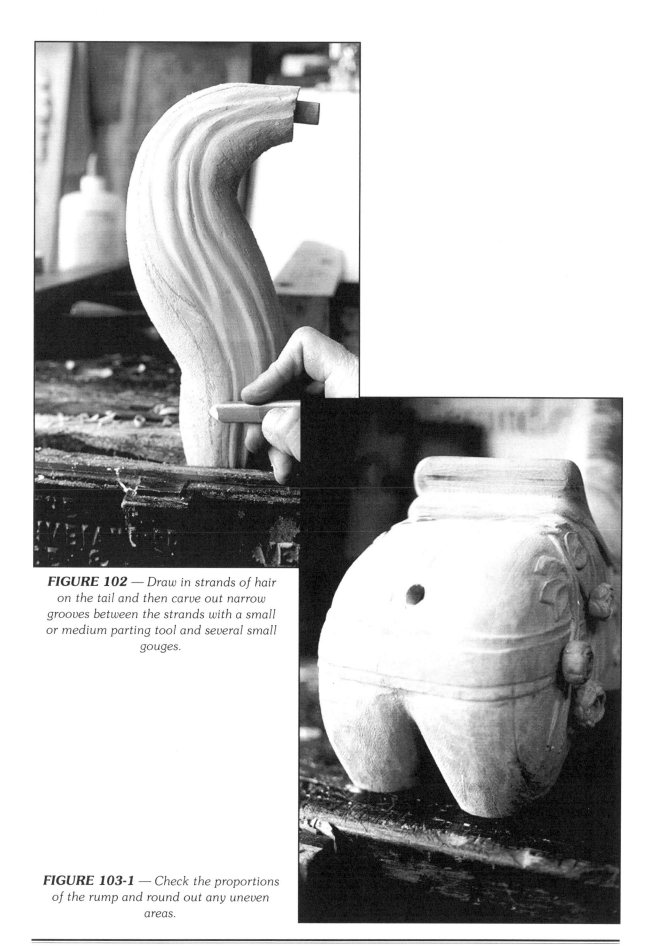

FIGURE 102 — *Draw in strands of hair on the tail and then carve out narrow grooves between the strands with a small or medium parting tool and several small gouges.*

FIGURE 103-1 — *Check the proportions of the rump and round out any uneven areas.*

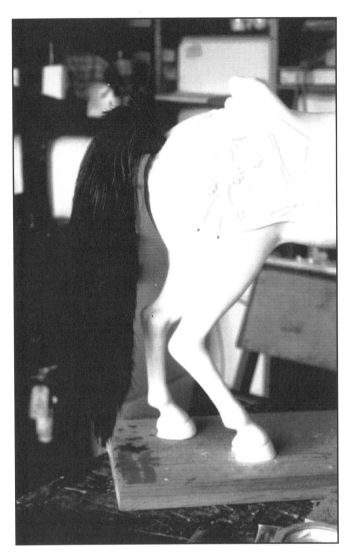

supply stores, particularly any that make leather equipment for mounted police or deputies, or riding clubs. If there are any horse ranches within reasonable distance of where you live, visit them and tell them what you have in mind.

Since you'll no doubt be inserting the tail in the rump to see how it looks (unless you're going to wait and try to get real horse hair), this is a good time for you to check the shape of the rump and decide if it needs more rounding or is okay the way it is right now. *(See Figures 103-1 and 103-2.)*

Figure 103-2 - Real horse hair can be used in place of a carved wooden tail.

♞ *CHAPTER V* ♞

PREPARING TO CARVE THE HEAD

The head is the most challenging part of the horse to carve. It calls for extra concentration and for paying attention to many details in a relatively small space. It'll keep you busy and frustrate you sometimes, but eventually a face, ears and a forelock will materialize before your eyes and hands.

A variety of tools can be utilized to carve the head. Such tools as medium gouges, small gouges, a V-parting tool, a chip carving knife, a draw knife, a coping saw, rifflers and medium and fine grit sandpaper. Sandpaper is lumped in along with the tools because it's such an integral part of the shaping process of the features and contours on the face, as well as other areas of the head.

You'll find yourself switching back and forth among the tools, as circumstances call for, in order to negotiate the planes and hollows and many details of the face. After the rough shape of the face is carved on the headpiece and you begin to feel more self-assured, start to work the various tools with your hands, especially for the finer carving. For the most part, you'll have much better control. And make sure that your tools are sharp, in case you haven't checked the cutting edges lately.

PRACTICE HEAD

The following recommendation, if taken, will help you considerably toward carving a beautiful head with a minimum of anxiety along the way. Instead of starting right out on the head you're planning to use on the horse, make a practice head. Make two practice heads. In fact, make as many practice heads as it takes for you to become less intimidated by the prospect of carving the final version of the head. If you're interested in making a practice head, here's how to go about it.

You'll need a half-dozen or so 1" thick lengths of soft wood at least 5" wide and about 10" long. Any type of cheap carving pine will do. For instance, pine shelving. If you have some thick chunks of soft wood lying around use them. Glue enough pieces together to make a block of wood approximating the thickness of the head, about $3\frac{3}{4}$" to 4" thick. In gluing up the wood, try to keep the bottom side, which will be the base of the head, as flat as possible. When the glue dries, place the head template against one side of the glued up wood. Draw an outline around the head template onto the practice head block. Then, saw out the practice head. If the bottom surface of the practice head is uneven, plane or sand it down to make it as flat as possible.

Next, saw off a 12" length from a two-by-four. Actually, any type of crude board with the same dimensions will do. Place the base of the head on one edge of the two-by-four with the nose facing out. Draw a pencil line across the edge of the two-by-four at the back of the head in order to line it up later.

Turn the head over and drill two holes straight down into the flat bottom surface of the practice head using a ½" diameter spade bit. Drill these holes about two inches apart and about three quarters of an inch deep. (If you have a pair of ½" diameter metal dowel centers that means you know how to use them, so skip to the next paragraph.)

Take a ½" diameter dowel and saw off two ½" long pegs. Place the head onto the two-by-four, using the pencil line you drew earlier as a reference mark. See that the dowel pegs are touching down in the middle of the edge of the board. Make a dot, or use an awl, to mark off the spots where the dowels are touching the wood.

Remove the head and drill two ½" diameter holes into the two-by-four where you made the two marks. Before gluing the practice head to the board, drill an eye hole in each side of the head with a ¾" diameter spade bit.

Spread glue on the edge of the two-by-four up to the pencil line. Squeeze a few drops into each hole. Turn the head over and spread glue along the length of the center area. Put a few drops into each hole also. Tap the dowels into the holes in the bottom of the head. Turn the head upright and maneuver the dowels into the holes in the board. Clamp the head to the board with whatever you have available: jaw clamp, bar clamp, wood handscrew or band belt. Wait the prescribed amount of time, then give it a little more time to make sure. When you're ready to carve, secure the board to your work surface and get ready to carve. (See Figure 104.)

COMMENTS BEFORE STARTING ON THE HEAD

Some of the photographs accompanying the instructions for carving out the face on the headpiece show only one side being worked on. It's best that you take a more balanced approach. After you make the initial cuts to shape the face on one side, repeat the cuts on the other side. Continue this approach throughout the carving of the face. Any fine bones, veins and other minute details, which you can choose to include on the face, are not described in the instructions. just the "meat and potatoes."

FIGURE 104 — Carving features on a practice head made from scrap wood may help to eliminate costly mistakes on the real head.

FACIAL EXPRESSION

Study closely the faces of the carousel horses created by the more masterly, revered carvers and you will occasionally notice distinctive expressions: anger, surprise, fear, gentleness and so on. For example, compare the mild, sensitive faces of many of Gustav Dentzel's horses to the barely restrained aggressiveness and fierceness depicted on the Stein and Goldstein horses.

The facial cast on most carousel horse faces usually includes the mouth, nostrils and eyes, and to some extent the ears, in varying degrees of suspended animation without any one feature dominating to reflect a mood or expression.

CARVING THE FACE

In the first stages of carving the face you can start out with either a draw knife, or a few large and medium shallow gouges. Although the draw knife works quickly in removing wood and establishing the basic planes, some people find it awkward to get used to. If you have the patience, however, and keep a sharp edge on the blade, you will find the draw knife to be an especially efficient and satisfying tool to use. It seems to conjure up a connective feeling with the old ways of working with wood.

If you're using a draw knife, begin by positioning the blade behind the eye hole. *(See Figure 105.)* Pull the blade forward, leaning it in at about a 30° angle. When the blade slices through the wood to approximately an inch in front of the eye hole, try to straighten out the blade, gliding it

FIGURE 105 — Carve away the sharp edges of the head with a draw knife.

along the side of the nasal bone. That's the bone that slants down the front of the face to the nostrils. (If you choose to carve the face with gouges, follow the same basic steps. Large gouges are good for gross cuts, and medium gouges should be used as you begin finer shaping.)

Pull the blade of the draw knife directly forward, but not all the way through. Instead, slack off and curve the blade outward near the front of the snout. If it seems like the wood wants to split, approach the cut from

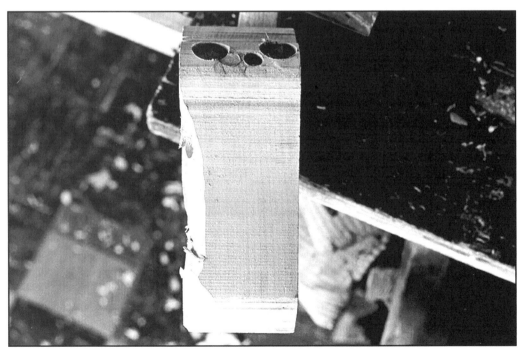

FIGURE 106 — Pull the blade outward toward the end of the nose. This movement will result in a curved cut along the top edge of the nose.

the opposite direction. To get a good idea of what you're attempting to accomplish, *see Figure 106*. Repeat the same procedure on the other side of the face before moving on.

Carve out the front corner of the snout with a large gouge or a draw knife. This cut should begin to curve outward about an inch or so above the upper lip. *(See Figure 107.)* Then, go over this curved surface a few times until it's relatively smooth and wide enough for you to later gouge out a nostril hole (on each side, of course).

If you were to observe a horse's face from a front view, you'd notice that the eyes are wider apart than are the nostrils. This distinction is not obvious in the photographs of carving

FIGURE 107 — *Using a large gouge or draw knife, carve out the front corner of the snout. This cut should begin to curve outward about 1" above the upper lip.*

the face, but you may be able to notice it in at least one of the face shots in the "Photo Gallery." Keep these structural relationships in mind as you carve so that the eyes and nostrils do not end up in a direct line with each other when viewed from the front. It's important, also, that you be aware of the gradual narrowing of the long snout as it tapers toward the nostrils. It's a matter of noodling around with the tools until you get it right, which is why making a practice head or two is worth the effort.

So far you've only carved along the top half of the side of the face. Go over the cuts you've made, this time using finer cuts so you don't overcarve. Let things evolve slowly to give yourself time to get accustomed to the more intricate carving involved in shaping the face. Try not to allow large chunks of wood to splinter off. You can't afford the luxury of casual butchering as you could when you were initially removing excess wood from the body. Before moving on, be sure to repeat on the other side of the face what you've done on the first side.

FIGURE 108 — *The chin is narrower than the upper part of the muzzle. To carve this area, use a draw knife and pull it forward along the chin.*

The chin is narrower than the upper part of the mouth and muzzle so that when viewed from the front the chin has a tapered look on each side. When shaping this area don't carve much beyond the back of the mouth along the side. If you're using a draw knife, begin by pulling the blade from the back of the mouth forward along the side of the face. *(See Figure 108.)* This example is from carving done on a practice head,

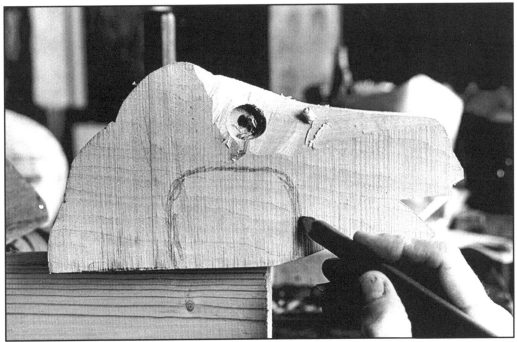

FIGURE 109-1 — *Draw a rounded rectangle on each side of the face to indicate the outline of the cheekbone.*

FIGURE 109-2 — *Remove the wood in front of the outline for the cheekbone with small, shallow cuts.*

which shows progress on the head further along than you probably are at this point. This may be the case in a few other instances. Actually, after the initial cuts have been made there's no strict order of things as far as carving the face goes. Don't be reluctant to move around.

Draw the outline of the cheekbone onto the wood. The profile of the cheekbone is a sort of rounded-off rectangle. Start carving into the area between the vertical line at the front of the cheekbone and the area in

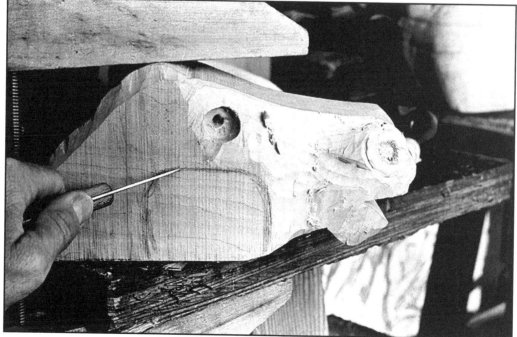

FIGURE 110 — *Score the outline of the cheekbone with a chip carving knife.*

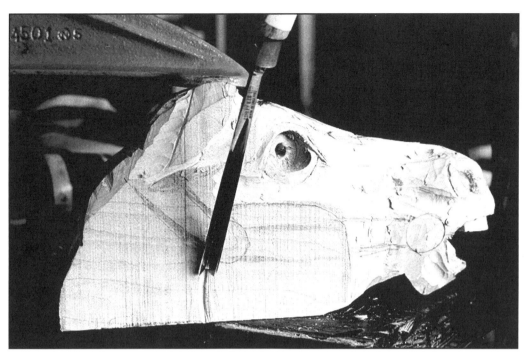

FIGURE 111-1 — *Following the score line, make a stop cut with a v-parting tool.*

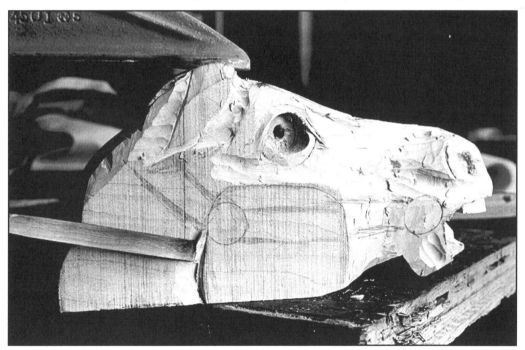

FIGURE 111-2 — *With a medium shallow gouge, remove small amounts of wood up to the stop cut.*

back of the mouth. *(See Figures 109-1 and 109-2.)* Keep the cuts shallow for now. You'll need the extra wood in order to carve the head straps.

Make a score line around the cheekbone outline with your chip carving knife. *(See Figure 110.)* At the back of the jawline, behind the cheekbone, make a stop cut with a V-parting tool along the vertical line. Then, with a medium shallow gouge carve in a horizontal direction from the neck, just back of the jawline, over to the vertical stop cut on the jawline.

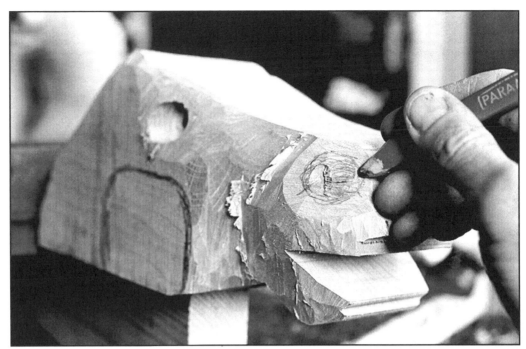

FIGURE 112-1 — *Draw a circle on each side of the nose to indicate the locations of the nostrils.*

FIGURE 112-2 — *Using a medium gouge, carve out a shallow hole inside the circle. Switch to a smaller gouge to make the hole deeper.*

Repeat this step until the back o the jaw is projecting out (not more than ¼") next to the recessed area behind it. *(See Figures 111-1 and 111-2.)*

NOSTRILS

Forewarned is forearmed. The nostrils are "killers" to carve for most

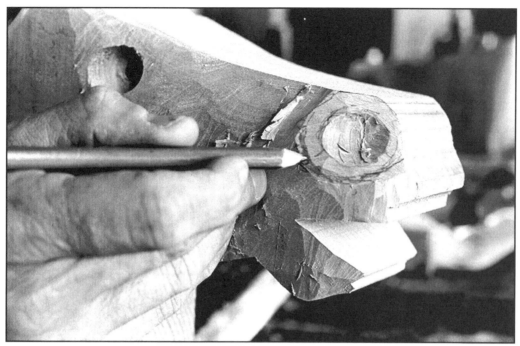

FIGURE 112-3 — *Draw a ring around the hole. This pencil line should be ³⁄₁₆" away from the edge of the hole, except at the top where it should be a little wider.*

people the first time around. Consider making a dry run or two on pieces of scrap wood or on a throw-away practice head.

Begin by drawing a circle about the size of a nickel on one side of the face where a nostril is going to be carved. Use a medium gouge to carve out a hole from the circle. When the hole has been started, give it a little more depth with a deeper and, if necessary, smaller gouge with the greater depth toward the front of the nostril. You can elongate the hole or

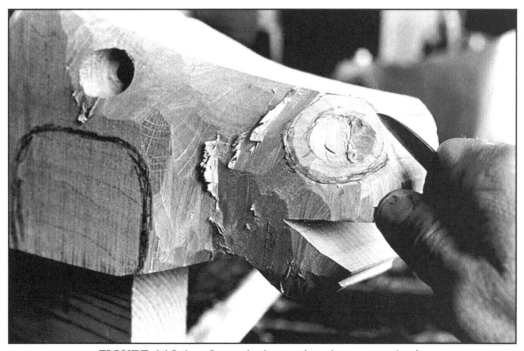

FIGURE 113-1 — *Score the line with a chip carving knife.*

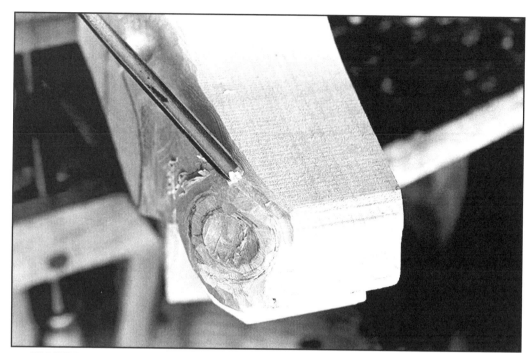

FIGURE 113-2 — *Gouge out a shallow trench around the ring just outside the score line.*

leave it round. Next, draw a ring around the nostril hole. The ring should be about ³⁄₁₆" from the edge of the hole, except at the top where it should be slightly wider. *(See Figures 112-1, 112-2 and 112-3.)* This additional width is for a particular carving detail which will be described in the next few pages.

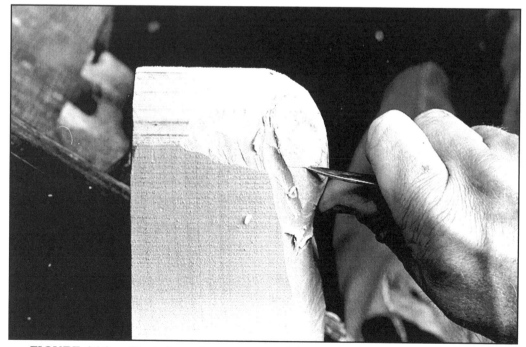

FIGURE 114 — *Start about three-quarters of the way back on the top of the nostril hole and make a stop cut with a chip carving knife across the nostril ring at a 45-degree angle.*

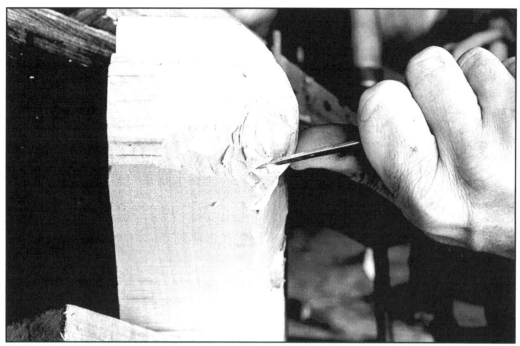

FIGURE 115-1 — *Cut down about ³/₁₆" deep to make a stop cut.*

FIGURE 115-2 — *Slice along the top of the nostril horizontally to meet the stop cut.*

Score the ring with your chip carving knife. Next, gouge out a shallow trench around the ring just outside the score line. Go all the way around the ring. *(See Figure 113-1 and 113-2.)*

You may be able to get a simplistic idea of what happens to the nostrils at the top by making an OK sign with your right hand. The traditional way to make this hand sign, of course, is to cover the top of the first joint on the index finger with your thumb. Let your thumb rest naturally over the top of the index finger. This finger-thumb configuration relates in a very basic way to the shape of a horse's nostril when open. If you try this and can't seem to visualize the relationship to a nostril hole, don't worry. Just flip to the close-ups in the "Photo Gallery" and you'll get the idea. When the nostril is open or slightly flared, the ringed area at the top of the nostril about three-quarters of the way back appears to trail back into the hole.

It can be a real head-scratcher until you take a close look at several variations of the nostrils in the open position. This will help you in figuring out how to carve them.

Starting about three-quarters of the way back on top of the nostril hole, make a stop cut with your chip carving knife across the nostril ring at about a 45° angle. *(See Figure 114.)*

Cut down about $3/16$" deep. Then, from the front, slice along the top of the nostril horizontally to meet the stop cut you made. *(See Figures 115-1 and 115-2.)*

Remove the wood you've sliced through. Next, make a stop cut at the point where the two cuts meet. This cut should start near the back and be angled slightly forward. Stop the cut when you cross over the top of the surface where you made the horizontal slice. With this cut you've begun to establish the overlap of the back part of the nostril. Ease into this cut, you don't want to slice through the narrow ledge of wood that's left at this point. *(See Figure 116.)* Again from the front, slice back along the *side* of the nostril ring to meet the last cut. *(See Figure 117.)*

Now it's a matter of making the lower part of the top of the nostril appear to be sliding back inside. You might have to gouge out some more

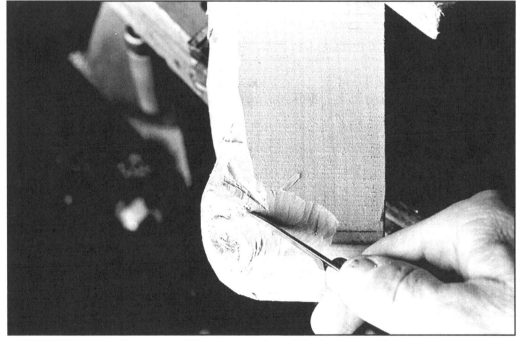

FIGURE 116 — *Start to establish the overlap of the back part of the nostril by making a stop cut at the point where the two cuts meet.*

FIGURE 117 — *Slice back along the side of the nostril ring to meet the stop cut.*

wood from the hole to do this. Maneuver the chip carving knife around until you manage to create this overlapping effect.

After both nostrils are started, draw a cone-like shape behind the nostril holes with a shallow gouge. Begin to emphasize the tapered flare of the nostrils by hollowing out a groove above and below the cone-like shape. (See Figure 118.)

Another detail to attend to is making sure there's a shallow groove

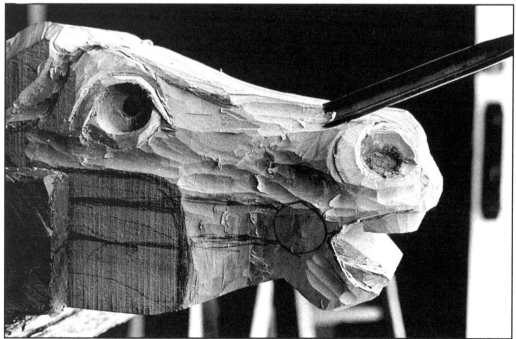

FIGURE 118 — *Hollow out a cone-shaped groove behind the nostrils with a shallow gouge.*

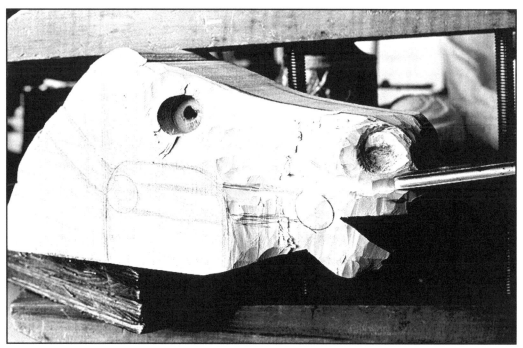

FIGURE 119 — *Carve a shallow groove under the nostrils with a small gouge.*

carved out under each nostril, if you haven't done so already. This groove should be carved with a small gouge. *(See Figure 119.)*

Leave enough room for the upper lip line, which still has to be established, when you begin working on the mouth. And yet another detail is the carving out and filing down of a little surface wood at the very front of the muzzle between the nostrils. Start carving where the muzzle begins to slope down toward the upper lip. This recessed span of wood will accent the flare of the nostrils.

Although the examples shown in the instruction photographs seem crude and exaggerated (because they are), this is pretty much the way the nostrils look in the preliminary stages. There are a number of variations of flared nostrils you can choose to carve. The specifics will have to be decided by you after you study carousel horse nostrils from your pictorial sources.

MOUTH

The mouth may seem to be the most complicated part of the face to carve, but it's not; just a bit of a tight squeeze getting inside is all. Begin by drawing a line along the side of the upper section of the teeth. This line will separate the upper lip from the upper teeth. Do the same with the lower teeth section. Here the line will not only separate the lip from the teeth, but also the tongue, as you'll soon find out. Each of the respective lines should be slightly curved rather than going straight back. *(See Figure 120.)* Repeat these lines on the other side, then join the lines in front of the mouth. The darkened area behind the upper front teeth, as shown in the photograph, will be sawed out.

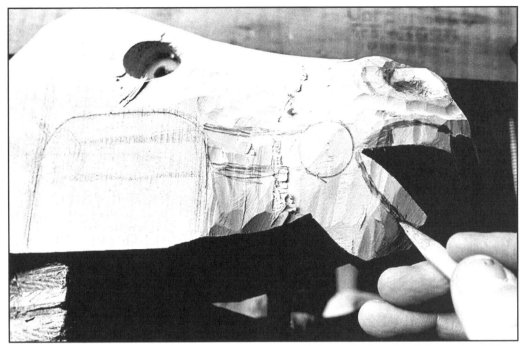

FIGURE 120 — *Draw on lines to separate the teeth from the lips. Both lines should be slightly curved toward the back of the mouth.*

Next, clamp the head in an upside down position. Draw a line across the back of the width of the upper teeth. Draw it about three-quarters of the way back from the front of the mouth. It's hard to get at this area with a pencil, so just do the best you can to mark a line. This line will serve as a guideline as you saw across the back area of the upper teeth.

Use a coping saw to cut out this back section. The goal is to create an

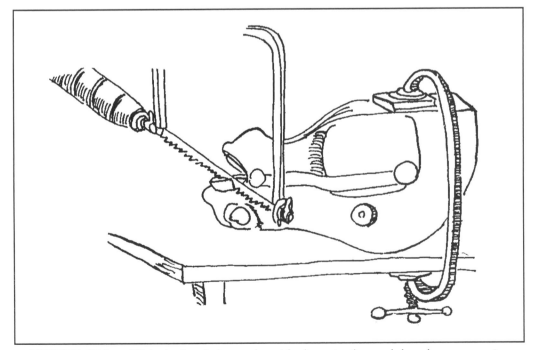

FIGURE 121 — *With the head clamped upside-down to the work bench, use a coping saw to cut the mouth.*

FIGURE 122 — *Turn the head up and reclamp it to the work bench. Score the line between the teeth and the lips deeply with a chip carving knife. Remove wood up to these stop cuts until the teeth are set in about ¼".*

open space. (On a real horse this space is referred to as the "bars" of the mouth where a bit can be placed.) Saw straight along the line until you reach the upper lip (mouth line). *(See Figure 121.)* Then, saw out the remaining wedge, starting from the back of the mouth and sawing forward.

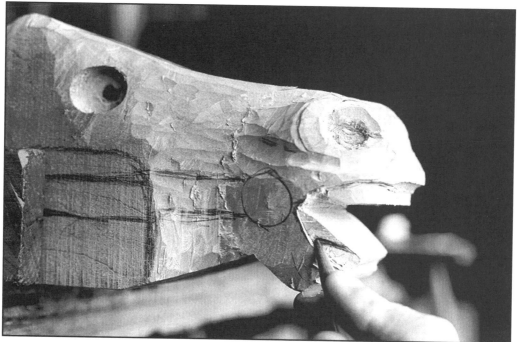

FIGURE 123 — *Draw a diagonal line on the side of the bottom teeth on both the left and the right sides. This line will mark where the tongue and the teeth meet.*

Now turn the head right-side up and clamp it to your work bench. Score the line between the teeth and lips with your chip carving knife until you've made fairly deep cuts. Begin slicing away thin layers of wood from the sides of both the upper and lower teeth sections until you reach the stop cuts. *(See Figure 122.)*

When the teeth are set in about ¼", draw a diagonal line along the side of the bottom teeth section, on each side. *(See Figure 123.)* The line should start at the outer tip of the teeth and slant back and down, ending at the midway point of the bottom of this lower section. This line will serve as a divider for the teeth and tongue. Score the line with your chip carving knife. *(See Figure 124.)* Slice away the surface of the wood that represents the side of the tongue. Go easy so you don't take off too much, too quickly.

Removing this wood will set the tongue in from the teeth the same way the teeth are set in from the lips. *(See Figure 125.)* As you're carving the teeth sections and the tongue, be sure to round off both the upper and lower corners of the front of the mouth.

The individual teeth are made by drawing lines separating each tooth, then carving out slivers of wood between each one. The upper teeth of a horse's mouth often have a moderate forward slant to them. On some carousel horses there is an extreme slant to the teeth. This seems to give the face an aggressive look. (On real horses, the older the horse, the more of a slant there is to the teeth.)

When you finish roughing out the teeth and tongue, make a shallow groove around the outside of the mouth about a ¼" above and below the edge of the mouth line. This groove will leave a lip line protruding around the mouth. At the front of the mouth both the upper and lower lips

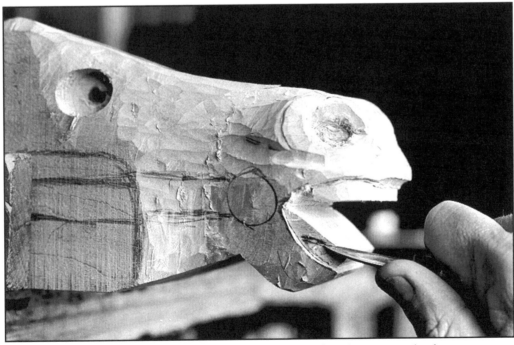

FIGURE 124 *— Score the diagonal line with a chip carving knife.*

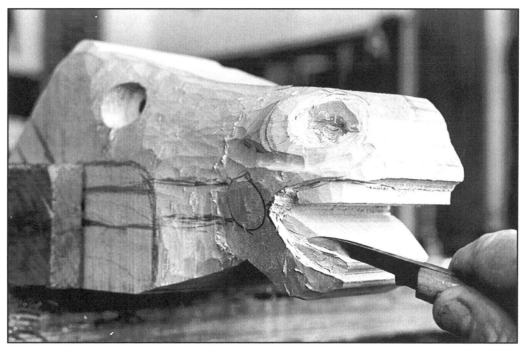

FIGURE 125 — *Slowly, remove the wood from the side of the tongue.*

protrude more than they do around the rest of the mouth. To make this protrusion, carve out or file off wood above the upper lip (carving from the nostrils down) and below the lower lip (carving from the chin up).

Take your time carving around the mouth, and occasionally check both sides to make sure everything is in balance. Folded-up sandpaper will come in very handy for the subtle shaping needed for the lips. Use rifflers for those hard-to-get-at places in the mouth.

EYES

Drilling eye holes in the head will initially limit your options in choosing an expression around the eyes. However, you can use wood epoxy or some other filler of your choice to alter the expression around the eyes, if you so wish, after you've started carving the eyelids. Another use for these kinds of materials is to build up the brow bone above each eye to achieve a certain expression or to fill in if you've overcarved in that area.

If it turns out, as the carving of the head progresses, that you drilled the eye holes too shallow or too deep, you can either drill the holes deeper with a $3/4$" diameter spade bit or fill in the holes with a very small amount of filler. You'll have to wait until carving on the head is well along before making that determination.

Because the insertion of the glass eyes brings such vitality and expressiveness to the face, there is sometimes an overwhelming desire to keep putting them into the holes and, with some effort, taking them out. This desire on the part of the carver is exceeded only by the desire of the eyes to bounce on the floor, where they usually become scratched or chipped. So try them once (assuming you've purchased a pair by now), get it out of your system, then wrap the eyes in a soft cloth or tissue and put them aside. If you have trouble getting the eyes out when you place them in the eye holes, try using a piece of tape with a strong adhesive, such as duct tape or electrician's tape, or even an elastic bandage. The important thing is not to scratch the surface of the eyes if at all possible.

One way of making it easier to slip the eyes in and out of the respective eye holes is to carve out a narrow, shallow slot in the upper half of the curve of the wood inside each eye hole. The tools that will probably help you the most are the chip carving knife and a small gouge or V-parting tool. When you get the slot started, a riffler can be used to work out some of the rough fibers. Don't make the slot too deep or the eyes will be rattling around in the holes. Later, the upper lids can be built up, or otherwise altered, with wood epoxy. Now, on to the detail carving around the eye holes.

Begin carving an eyelid around one of the eye holes by making a downward cut with your chip carving knife on each side of the eye at the midway point. *(See Figure 126.)*

This is the first step in separating the eyelids. Carve out a sliver of wood from each cut, slicing upward from the bottom. These cuts will represent the corners of the eye. Next, draw a line about $1/4$" above the top half of the eye hole following the curved line of the hole. *(See Figure 127.)* Bring the line down to where the stop cuts end on each side. Then draw a curved line below, following the lower half of the eye hole.

Score both of the curved lines above and below the eye hole. Carve out a sliver of wood from the outside edges of the respective eyelids,

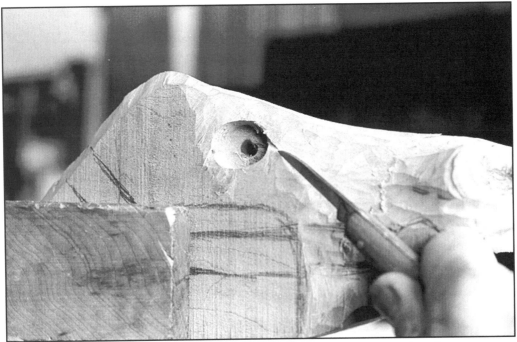

FIGURE 126 — *To carve the eyelids, first make a downward cut with a chip carving knife on each side of the eye at the midway point.*

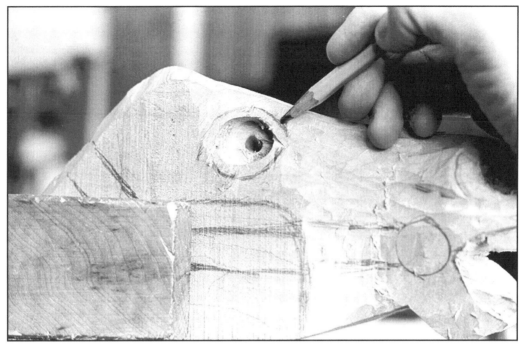

FIGURE 127 — *Draw a curved line ¼" above the eye and another curved line ¼" below the eye.*

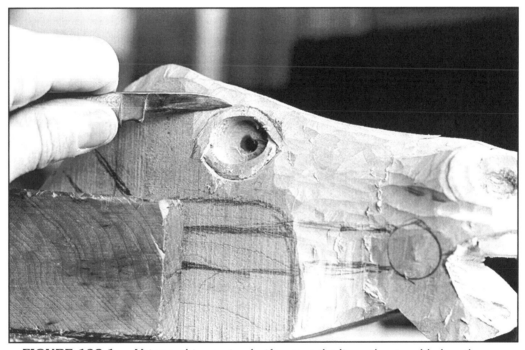

FIGURE 128-1 — *Using a chip carving knife, score the lines above and below the eye.*

following the scored lines. *(See Figures 128-1 and 128-2.)* Begin shaping the eyelids based on what you've seen in photographs and from whatever sources you've been using in addition to pictures.

The eyes on some carousel horses show the upper lid overlapping the lower lid at each corner. Others show the upper lid overlapping the lower lid only at the back corner with a notch-like cut at the front corner of the

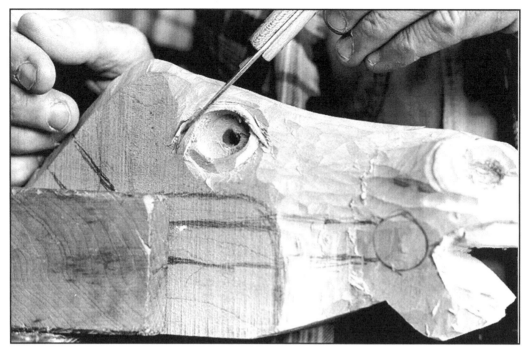

FIGURE 128-2 — *Carve out a sliver of wood from the outside of the stop cut to raise the eyelids.*

eye, similar to the average human eye when relaxed. This notch cut is the eyelid shape seen on the eyes of many of the more popular standard-sized carousel horses. To get an idea of what this cut looks like, turn ahead to *Figures 157-1 and 157-2.* Carving these details will be another case of personal choice according to what style you prefer.

When you're close to finishing the horse, meaning before it is painted, the glass eyes can be glued in with an epoxy glue or whatever you have around that binds glass to wood. Of course, you can always insert them in a less permanent way with two-way adhesive tape or by simply pressing them in and seeing if they will stay firmly in place, yet can still be removed without using a great deal of force. This method depends on variables such as the degree to which you've made modifications to the pre-drilled eye holes.

In order to protect the eyes, you can coat them with a clear rubber cement or dab on a clear varnish. Make sure that whatever material you use to protect the eyes can be removed later with a prescribed solution without scratching up the surface of the eyes.

The eyes can also be inserted after the horse has been painted. This way requires that you pre-determine the relative ease with which the eyes can be inserted and, if necessary, removed from the holes. When the paint is thoroughly dry you can glue in the eyes or just press them in.

COMPLETING THE HEAD

Before getting to the task of carving the ears, several details need to be covered regarding the completion of the head. Let's begin with the area

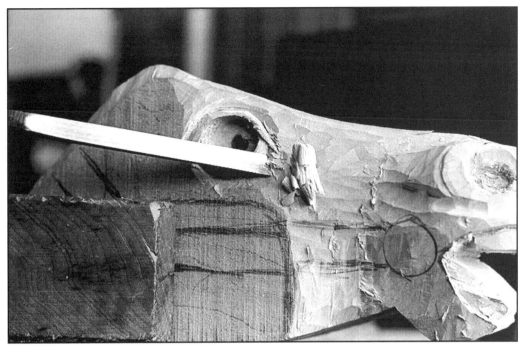

FIGURE 129 — *Using a medium shallow gouge or a medium chisel, gently taper the wood in front of the eye toward the side of the nose.*

just in front of each eye, which is often avoided at this stage due to uncertainty as to what to do about it. What you can do is take a medium shallow gouge or a medium chisel and shave the wood off in a gradual taper toward the side of the long nasal area. This is a subtle bit of tapering. *(See Figure 129.)*

Next, carve out a channel, or groove, between the bottom of the eye

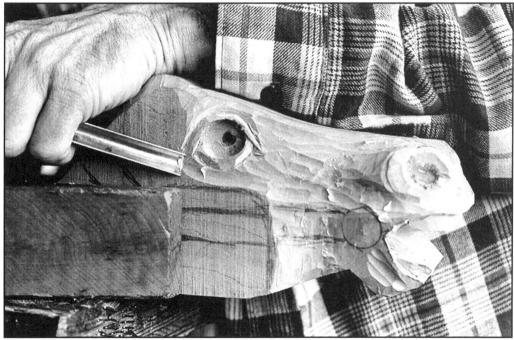

FIGURE 130 — *To accent the top of the cheekbone, carve a groove between the bottom of the eye and the top of the cheekbone with a medium gouge.*

FIGURE 131-1 — *Draw an outline of the forelock on the top of the head.*

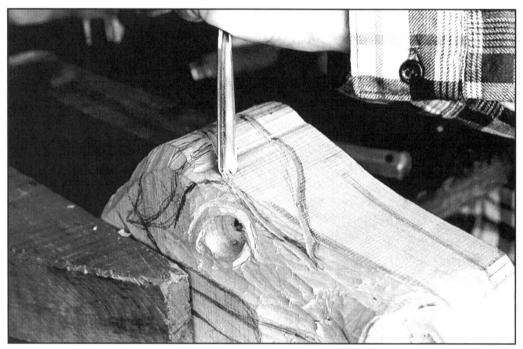

FIGURE 131-2 — *Score the line with a medium or small v-parting tool.*

and the top of the cheekbone. A medium gouge like a #11 (10mm) or #9 (7mm) can be used to carve out this groove, which will sharply accent the top of the cheekbone. *(See Figure 130.)*

That odd-looking bump on top of the head, which gives a distortion to the profile, is there for a good reason—that being in case you want to carve a high forelock on the brow. (The forelock is the hair that falls over the brow.) If not, just carve it down to where you want it. You're better off

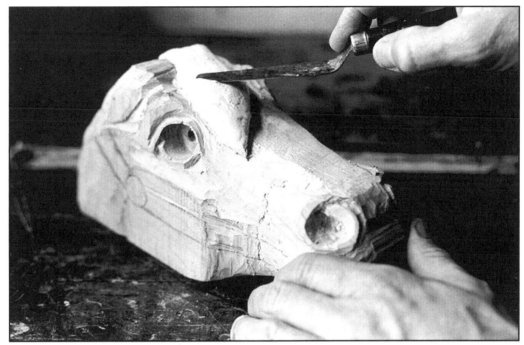

FIGURE 132 — *To build up the forelock, use wood epoxy or some other filler on the top of the head. This step is optional.*

waiting until after you've started on the forelock outline before carving down the exaggerated height.

First, decide where you want the forelock to fall on the brow, and whether or not part of it will swing back around one of the ears. Then, draw a forelock onto the wood. Score around the forelock with a medium or small V-parting tool. *(See Figures 131-1 and 131-2.)*

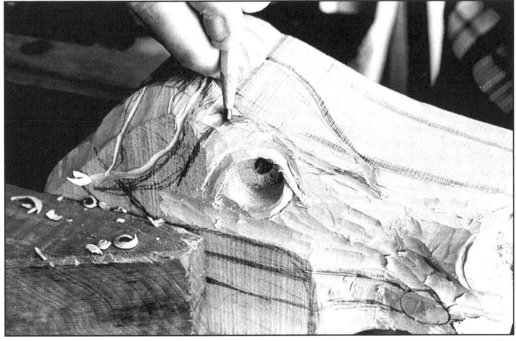

FIGURE 133-1 — *Make a raised brow bone over each eye by drawing a curved line ½" above the eye.*

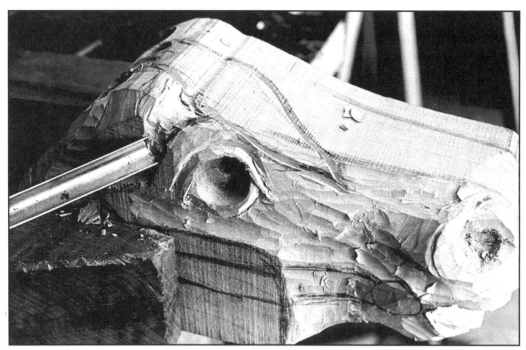

FIGURE 133-2 — *Rough out the basic shape of the brow by removing wood from behind the pencil lines.*

Carve out a thin layer of wood from around the outer surface of the forelock. Don't go too deeply at first. As you work on the forelock, redraw the lines for the nasal bone (the parallel lines extending down the face from the front of the eyes to the nostrils as shown in *Figures 131-1 and 131-2*) if they're carved or sanded off. If you want to build up the forelock or otherwise make additions, apply wood epoxy or some other filler to raise it up from the head. *(See Figure 132.)*

Begin making a raised brow bone over each eye by drawing a curved line about ½" above the eye up to where the forelock is scored. If the forelock you're carving is narrow and in the middle of the brow, then follow the curvature of the brow bone as it would naturally arch above the eye and dip down on each end. Scoop out some wood from behind the pencil line you've drawn using a medium gouge. Don't overcarve, just rough out the basic shape you want. *(See Figures 133-1 and 133-2.)*

If you haven't started on the headstraps yet, now is as good a time as any to begin. Draw the style you want, plain or fancy, onto the wood. Score the straps with your chip carving knife, then make stop cuts over the score marks with a V-parting tool. (You can also use a small gouge to carve away a thin layer of wood up to the score marks.) Keep repeating these steps until you've gradually removed enough wood so that the straps are standing out in relief. *(See Figures 134-1 and 134-2.)*

Make good use of rifflers and sandpaper to get the straps established in relief. The primary concern is to get at least a carved outline of the straps started, if nothing more at this point.

You should also include a brow strap across the top of the head. *(See*

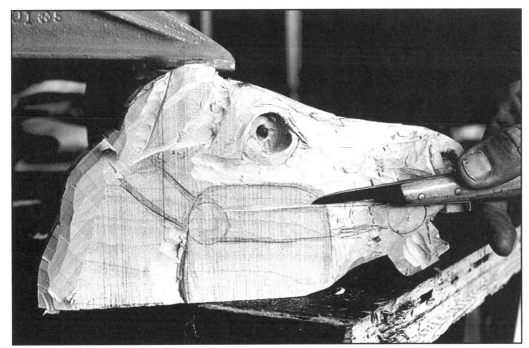

FIGURE 134-1 — *Draw straps on the face and score the lines with a chip carving knife. Make stop cuts over the score marks with a v-parting tool.*

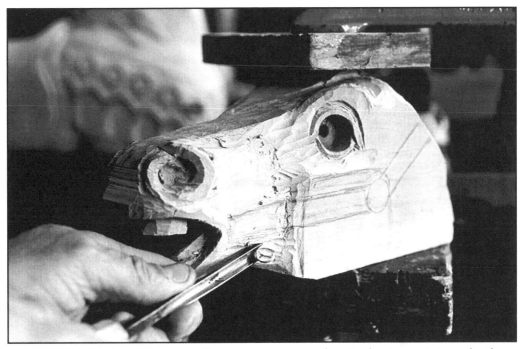

FIGURE 134-2 — *Using a small gouge, remove wood up to the stop cuts to make the straps stand out in relief.*

Figure 135.) This strap is not shown in some of the photographs of the preliminary carving stages on the head.

At the back of the head on the right side begin carving off the sharp corners that will soon become part of the mane. On the left side, start carving out a groove to show a clear separation of the mane from the neck. *(See Figures 136-1 and 136-2.)*

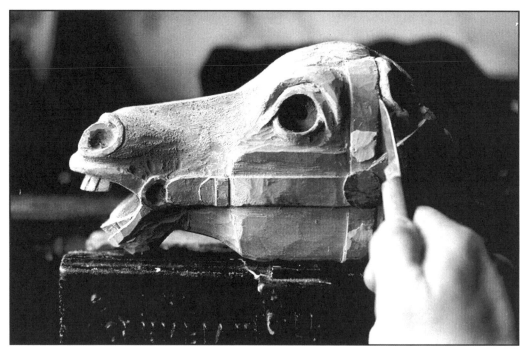

FIGURE 135 — *Include a brow strap across the head. Relieve it from the head by making stop cuts and removing wood with a small gouge.*

There's another detail you can choose to include in the carving on the head, although if you choose not to hardly anyone will notice. There are two protrusions of bone in the lower jaw that run parallel along the length of the underside of the jaw on each side. These two bones stop short of the chin pouch. *(See Figure 137.)* Use a small or medium deep gouge to carve out the respective grooves just to the inside of the "bones," and a

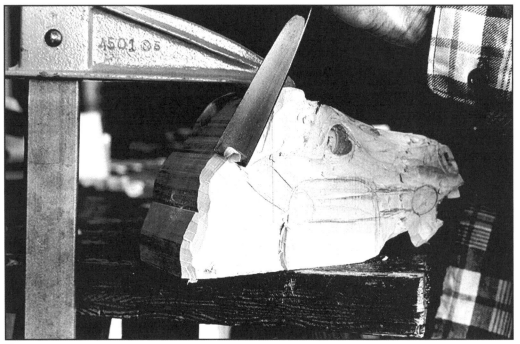

FIGURE 136-1 — *On the right side at the back of the head, carve off the sharp corners of the mane.*

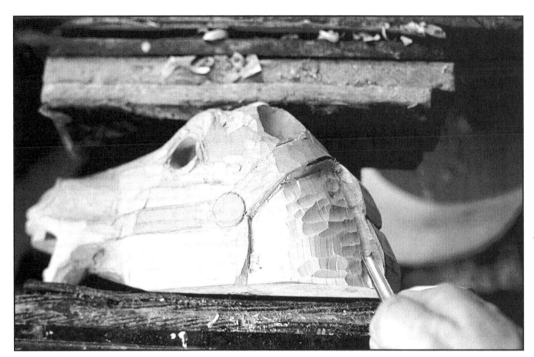

FIGURE 136-2 — *On the left side, carve a groove to separate the mane from the neck.*

FIGURE 137 — *Use a small or medium deep gouge to carve out grooves to show the bones under the chin. This step is optional.*

shallow medium gouge to carve out the middle recessed area. There is a photograph in the "Photo Gallery" that partially shows the underside of the jaw.

Finally, direct your attention to the nostrils, which need some additional definition. Begin by scooping out more wood above and below the sides of the nostrils back to where the cone-like shapes taper off. Emphasizing the flare of the nostrils adds more character and spirit to the face. Sandpaper will help considerably in shaping the flare of the nostrils.

EARS

You might find it of some interest to know that on a real horse it is not the eyes, the mouth or the nostrils that are the most expressive in terms of registering reactions to stimuli; it's actually the ears. This little bit of information will have no bearing on how you carve any of these parts, it just seems to be worth letting you know as you go about the business (or pleasure) of carving the face and the rest of the head. Now let's begin carving out two of these sensitive little radar beacons.

A chip carving knife is the primary tool that should be used for carving the ears. Consider wearing an elastic bandage or a rubber thimble on the thumb of your carving hand if you're not comfortable yet with the chip carving knife. This part of the carving requires constant attention as to where your fingers are in relation to the cutting edge of the knife. So please be careful.

Before getting underway, a word about this particular method of carving the ears. You may be wondering why the ears were not just in-

FIGURE 138-1 — *Carve the ears from a piece of scrap wood or a dowel. Use a chip carving knife to create a sloping surface.*

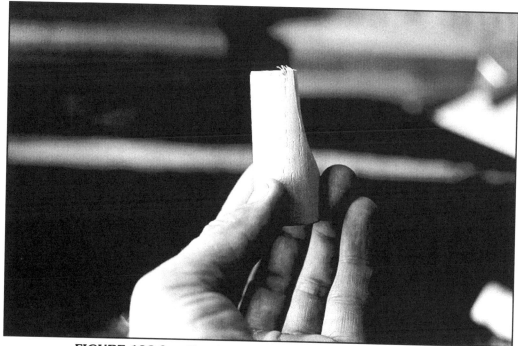

FIGURE 138-2 — The sloping surface will be the front of the ear.

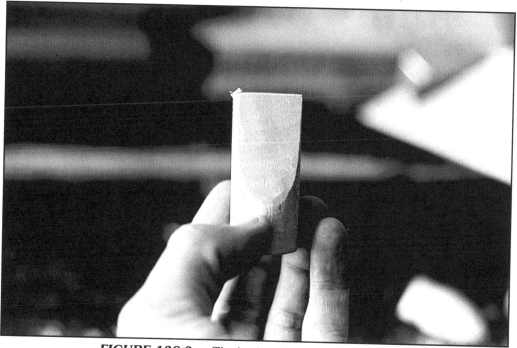

FIGURE 138-3 — The back of the ear will be rounded.

cluded as part of the head piece when it was sawed out. It's certainly one way of being able to carve the ears, that is as part of the head. But carving the ears as two portable units allows you to carve with the grain since the ears, on this particular design, are set in an upright position (which is against the grain direction of the head.) Also, if you mess up one of the ears you can always make up another one out of a piece of carving wood or from a soft pine dowel, if you can locate an outlet that sells them.

First, mark an "R" for right on the bottom of one ear piece, and "L"

FIGURE 139-1 — *Leave a small square at the top of the ear.*

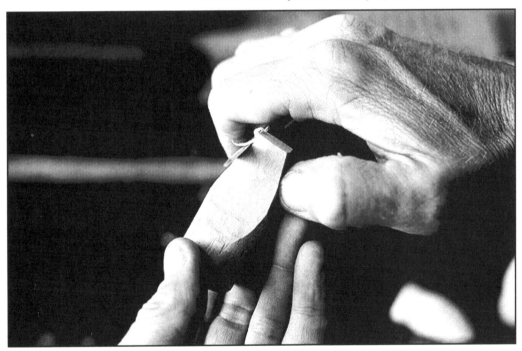

FIGURE 139-2 — *Angle the sides up toward the top of the ear.*

for left on the other one. Next, cut a slice in the side of one of the ear pieces about three-quarters of the way down. Then, angle the direction of the knife blade upward and carve out a long sloping surface. *(See Figures 138-1, 138-2 and 138-3.)* This surface is going to be the front of the ear from which the cavity will be carved. Midway up the length of the *back* of the ear start slicing up toward the top. Make a rounded curve as you carve upward, but don't carve so far over that you meet the first cut at the top. Not yet. Instead, leave a width of about ¼" or more

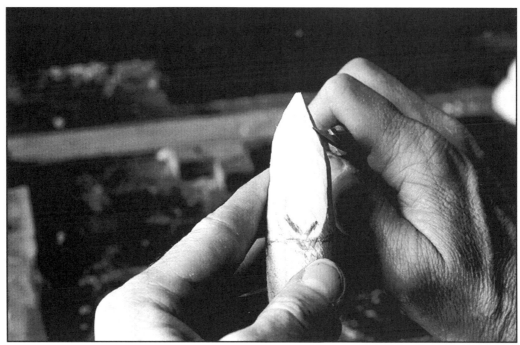

FIGURE 140 — Define the convex shape of the outer edge of the horse's ear. The inside edge is convex at the bottom and curves in toward the top.

at the top to allow for maneuvering room as you shape the rest of the ear.

On the sides, beginning at the midway point, carve over toward the top. Leave a small square at the top. *(See Figures 139-1 and 139-2.)* Now on to finer details.

The contour of a horse's ear on the outer side, in an upright position, has a slight convex shape for the most part. The inner side starts out

FIGURE 141 — Draw a "V" at the bottom of the ear where the ear cavity will start.

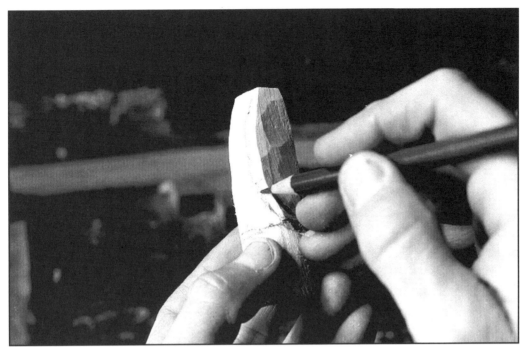

FIGURE 142 — Draw a second line starting ¼" outside the bottom of the "V" mark and ending at the top of the ear. Draw an identical line on the other side. The two lines should meet at the top of the ear.

convex, but near the top it curves in and becomes concave, (this describes the ear from a front view). This basic shape needs to be established before moving on to the next step of the carving. *(See Figure 140.)*

Once you have a good start on roughing out these contours, begin rounding off the back area. Keep working around the ear and shaving off some of the surface wood, a little at a time. Go back over the concave

FIGURE 143 — Score the lines on each side of the ear to make a stop cut.

and convex shapes on the sides and gradually carve up toward the top until a point emerges.

Insert the ear you're working on into the hole it will eventually go into permanently. Draw a circle all the way around the bottom of the ear. Remove the ear and draw a V on the front surface where the cavity will be carved out, just above the circle. *(See Figure 141.)* Now make a stop cut around the circle with your chip carving knife. Carve out a very narrow groove above it all the way around. This little groove will give you a stopping point as you continue shaping the ear.

At the bottom of one side of the V mark, draw a line about $\frac{1}{4}$" outside the mark all the way to the top. Draw along the side of the front edge of the ear. *(See Figure 142.)* Repeat this procedure on the other side of the ear. The lines should meet at the top, behind the point of the ear. Score these lines on each side of the ear. Go over them again to make a good stop cut. Carve out a sliver of wood along the length of the stop cut. *(See Figure 143.)* If you should decide to use a V-parting tool instead of a chip carving knife, be sure to clamp down the ear so that both of your hands are free. Do not steady the ear with one hand while using a V-parting tool with the other. The small size and rolly shape of the ear make it very easy for the piece to slip out of your grasp. At any rate, the lines along the edge of the ear, when carved out, will leave a rim of wood that will represent the cartilage around the outside of the ear cavity. *(See Figure 144.)*

There's a subtle curvature on the front surface of the ear, which is a touch you can add if you choose to. *(See Figures 145-1 and 145-2.)* If you don't, the overall shape of the ear will not be diminished. The two photographs show the ear as seen from the top.

FIGURE 144 — *Remove a sliver of wood along the stop cut to represent the cartilage around the outside of the ear cavity.*

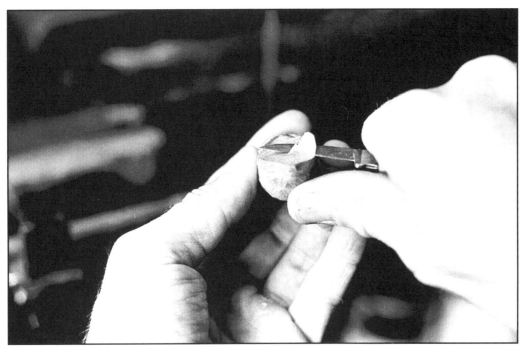

FIGURE 145-1 — *Using a chip carving knife, add a subtle curvature to the front of the ear.*

FIGURE 145-2 — *This curvature is so slight that the overall shape of the ear will not be diminished if it is omitted.*

Next, clamp the ear so that the front surface is facing up. Begin scooping out wood to create a cavity. Start at the bottom of the V mark using a V-parting tool. After making the initial cut into the wood, you can either continue working with the V-parting tool or use a medium gouge to finish scooping out the cavity. The cavity should be made increasingly shallow as you near the top of the ear, about half-way up. *(See Figure 146.)*

FIGURE 146 — *Use a v-parting tool or a medium gouge to scoop out the wood inside the ear cavity. The cavity should be shallower at the top of the ear.*

As you're carving out the cavity you'll find a tendency for the wood to splinter. When this occurs reverse directions with the gouge. And don't carve too close to the edges, at first. The remainder of the carving of the ear involves cleaning up and refining to get the desired shape you want. *(See Figures 147-1 and 147-2.)*

The other ear is carved the same way as the first with the exception of the contours on the sides which are reversed, meaning the slight concave

FIGURE 147-1 — *Clean up and refine the ear to get the final shape.*

FIGURE 147-2 — *The other ear is carved in the same fashion as the first ear, but the outside curves of the ear are reversed.*

shape at the top half of the ear you carved first goes on the opposite side of the other ear.

Wood filler, speckle or wood epoxy can be used to cover the seam around the bottom of each ear where it shows after the ears have been glued into the holes.

♞ *CHAPTER VI* ♞

FINISHING UP

Temporarily assemble the horse again and check over your progress. Make any necessary markings on the various parts where they join up so they can be blended together through additional carving. On the head, mark the edges of the wood that extend beyond the thickness of the neck section on the body. *(See Figure 148.)* This will let you know how much carving needs to be done in order for the head section to join evenly with the body. Finish the mane by adding on the segments that need to be carved on the headpiece.

Now is a good time to create any nuances around muscled areas such as the hindquarters, shoulders and upper legs. Rifflers and sandpaper play a significant role in finishing up details. Start with a coarse or medium grit sandpaper, depending on the

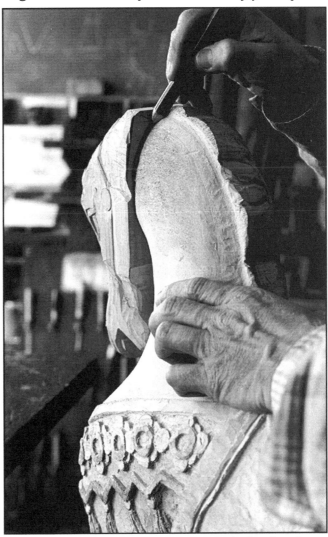

FIGURE 148 — *Temporarily attach the head to the neck. Trace the outline of the neck onto the head. This pencil line will act as a guideline for removing wood from the area where the head joins the neck.*

---

condition of the wood surface in any particular area, and work your way up to finer grades.

Remember, this is another temporary attachment. Do *not* glue the parts together prematurely. When you're through making the necessary markings for adjustments, you can unscrew the legs and the head from the body and continue with the fine-shaping. Or, you might find it more practical to leave the horse attached as a unit for a while as you make refinements. If you're still far from being finished on much of the carving, it's best to continue working on the various parts separately. This is especially true if any modifications need to be made on the legs and, particularly, the head. *(See Figures 149-1 and 149-2.)* Don't put your chip carving knife away yet, you may still need to go over the eyelids, teeth and forelock strands.

If you plan on painting the horse, it isn't necessary to go beyond 120-grit sandpaper on the bare wood. When you're through sanding and you apply sanding sealer (and later a few undercoats), you can sand over these coats lightly using 150-grit sandpaper. There's no need to go up to 220-grit sandpaper or other very fine grades; that's overdoing it when you're going to cover the wood with paint.

Due to the fact that basswood is such a bland, uninteresting wood, nothing will be mentioned about staining it beyond suggesting that you not do it.

GLUING THE PARTS TOGETHER

Glue the legs to the body whenever you think you're far enough along.

FIGURE 149-1 — *Carve the base of the head so the head and neck blend together seamlessly. Complete any fine shaping before attaching the head to the body permanently.*

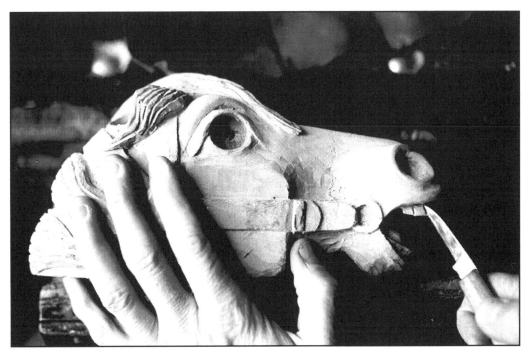

FIGURE 149-2 — Add details to the teeth with a chip carving knife.

If the holes have become enlarged to the point that the screws are not solidly secured into the holes, plug up the holes in the body with short lengths of $^1/_8"$ diameter dowel pieces. You could also just drill the holes larger and use a corresponding diameter dowel size to plug up the holes.

Measure the length you'll need by inserting the dowel, of whatever diameter you decide to use, and marking the spot where you will saw the piece off. Remove the dowel, or dowels, and saw the piece off. Rub glue on the dowel pegs and squeeze a drop or two into the screw holes. Next, tap the dowel pegs into the respective holes. When the glue dries, file or sand off any roughness around the glued up area. Place the leg or head against the surface on the body where it will be joined. Then, using a $^1/_8"$ diameter drill bit, insert the bit through the hole in the part to be attached and re-drill the screw holes.

In case the heads of the #10 roundhead screws have become stripped or flawed in any other way, buy new screws before gluing everything together. You don't want to run into problems with the screws when the glue has been spread on the wood and you're ready to permanently attach the legs and head to the body. Be sure to use washers with the screws; it makes a difference in locking the screws in place more securely. Use yellow glue, or as a second choice, white glue for the final assembling. If you use white glue give it plenty of time to set up properly, at least overnight. When you apply the glue, smear it around liberally on both surfaces, then wipe off the excess as the pressure you apply to tighten the screws forces the glue out.

You'll probably be nit-picking away on the head until the very end, so don't feel compelled to glue it on immediately. It depends on where you are with it. When you do get around to gluing the head permanently to the body, be sure to use a washer for a solid grip.

Securing the tail is a matter of gluing a dowel peg into the hole in the tail, then squeezing glue into the tail hole in the body. Be sure to smear glue around on the two surfaces that will rest against each other. Use a few thick rubber bands or doubled over strips of tied-together old tire tubes for holding the tail securely to the body as the glue dries.

PATCHING AND FILLING IN

Several commercial wood fillers are available for patching, filling in and building up specific areas on the horse, if needed. *(See Figure 150.)*

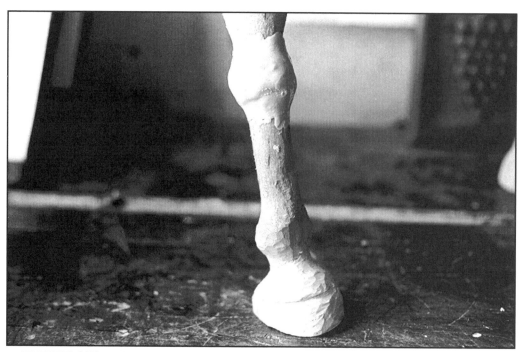

FIGURE 150 — *Wood fillers can be used to build up areas that may have been carved too thin, such as the legs and the neck.*

These products are useful in cases where you may have carved part of a leg too thin, trimmed the neck down thinner at the base than you intended to, scooped out too much wood from the seat of the saddle and other such instances where filler is needed. Sometimes filler is used just to conceal minor flaws or to cover up seams where two parts have been joined.

Wood epoxy is a good type of wood filler. This product can be carved, filed, sanded and painted after it has dried thoroughly, and is superior to many other filler and patching compounds. It often comes in two containers, the contents of which are of a thick pasty consistency. Each time there's a need to make repairs or build up an area, equal portions of the ingredients from each container are mixed together and spread on with a palette knife or any kind of flat, thin metal implement that is sturdy and flexible enough for applying this substance. When the mixture is ready, it can be crudely molded to the shape desired, but it must be completely dry before any carving can be done on it. (This material does have a "shelf life." And, it will harden if the lids are left off or not screwed on tightly.)

Unless you're planning to make several horses within a short period of time, buy a set of *pint size* containers, rather than quart size. Otherwise, you'll find yourself stuck with a large amount of filler that you may not use for a long time.

If you know of a similar product, by all means give it a try. As far as standard commercial fillers, you're advised to use caution when purchasing such products. Many of these filler and patching products are brittle to work with when dry and are not satisfactory to carve on details.

Use speckling paste to fill in and cover any rough wood fibers in places like the nostrils, or in any other places that you just can't seem to sand any smoother. It's also good for covering minor seams and smoothing over any problems around the trappings. This light patching material is described in "Miscellaneous Tools and Materials" at the beginning of the book.

JEWELS

If you plan to put jewels on the horse, a good size to use is 20mm ($5/8$") in diameter. This size looks good on the body trappings of a small horse. A $5/8$" spade bit seems logical for a jewel that size, but you may find the hole it makes is too large. The size of the glass jewels as specified for a certain diameter are not always consistent for that size. A $9/16$" bit, although slightly smaller, will let you control the gradual enlargement of the holes. Drill holes in scrapwood first to try the jewels for an accurate fit. Fasten the jewels securely with clear epoxy glue or any other strong adhesive that bonds glass and wood. Try to use flat-backed glass jewels.

PAINTING THE HORSE

A few types of paints to choose from are as follows: acrylics, oils and enamels (oil-based). Colored stains can also be applied, but with basswood you'll still be working with wood that's about as interesting as vanilla ice cream. Unfortunately, there is no carousel horse painting book available to refer you to. However, there are a few articles in back issues of *Carrousel Art Magazine* that discuss the painting of carousel animals. Another thing you might do is write to a few carousel organizations and ask them for the names of any individuals or publications that can help provide you with information concerning special painting techniques.

The prospect of painting your horse can be a real anxiety producer. Certainly no one wants to take a quality carving job and cover it with a mediocre paint job. So it's probably going to be helpful if you practice first on some scrap wood or on other leftover parts such as a practice head. Another approach you can take in getting the horse painted is to hire a professional artist to do the job, one who works with tube oils. The tube oils can be applied over an *oil-based* enamel undercoat. Of course a proposition such as this could turn out to be a costly commission job, unless you're acquainted with an artist willing to work out a mutually agreeable arrangement. For instance, you could promise to clean up all his or her paint brushes for the next twenty years in exchange for the paint job of a lifetime.

Whatever you decide about painting your horse, read the next few pages before actually starting on it. And take advantage of the copy pattern in the pattern section at the end of this book. Make several copies with either tracing paper or photocopies. Use the copies to come up with a color scheme, through trial and error, that can be used as a guide for painting the horse.

BRASS SLEEVE

A practical decision that needs to be made soon is whether or not you want the horse to have a pole going through it. The word "pole" is a misnomer, in this case, because poles normally used on carousel horses are hollow brass tubes referred to as brass sleeves. On standard-sized carousel horses, these brass sleeves are often slipped over a slightly smaller diameter black steel pole that runs all the way through the body into a flange secured to the floor. The brass sleeve does not usually run all the way through the body, but rests on top of the pommel or the withers. Another section of brass sleeve is then slipped onto the bottom half of the

FIGURE 151 — *Before painting the horse, decide if a pole will be added to the finished carousel horse.*

steel pole, the part that emerges from beneath the animal. In fact, the main purpose of the brass sleeve is to cover up a lackluster black pole inside the sleeve. (You now know more about poles and brass sleeves than you thought there was to know and, in fact, probably care to know.)

Because your horse is considerably smaller and lighter than the standard carousel horses, the brass sleeve/steel pole combination is uncalled for. All you need is one section of brass sleeve running through the horse. *(See Figure 151.)*

If you can't locate a brass sleeve, or afford one, a solid steel pole can be used, or you could even use a 1" diameter dowel or broomstick. All you'll need to do is paint whatever alternative you choose to use with a gold-colored paint or a gold bronzing powder mixed with varnish so that it resembles brass. Keep in mind that you *don't* have to drill a hole through the horse and insert a brass sleeve or a pole; the horse can be made to stand on three hooves on a base unassisted by a shaft of any kind. This alternative will be covered later.

First, let's consider the insertion of a brass sleeve. For a horse the size of the one on which you've been working, a 1" diameter brass sleeve seems to work best. A 2" diameter sleeve is just too big; it's best suited for some of the larger animals. A ½" diameter sleeve is too spindly looking. A ¾" sleeve would be j-u-u-st right, but try to find one with a matching diameter finial. A finial is a brass cap or spire that fits atop the brass sleeve. Anyway, the brass sleeve that is the most natural looking, proportionally speaking, is the 1" diameter size, which is fairly easy to come by.

There are two basic types of brass

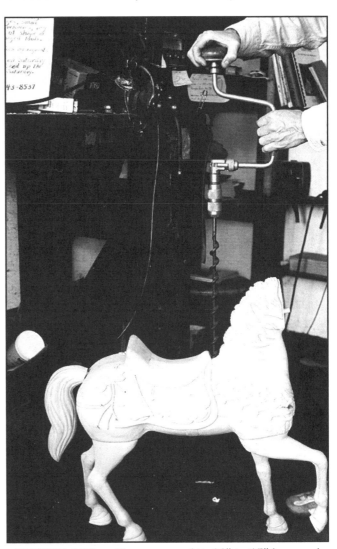

FIGURE 152 — *Use an auger bit, 12" to 15" long and 1" in diameter, to drill a hole through the body of the horse.*

sleeves inserted through carousel animals. One type is referred to as a "twisted" brass sleeve. This type has an unbroken spiral groove cut along the length of the metal. The other type is a plain brass sleeve. By far, the first type is the more attractive and fanciful of the two. You can also look in your local telephone book under "Brass" or "Lamps."

DRILLING THE HOLE
THROUGH THE BODY—OR NOT

Choosing the best way to secure your horse is an important decision to make after coming this far on the carving, so read over the following procedures before deciding.

Drilling a hole through the body, if you're planning to go that route, means that you'll have to start exercising your "squinting" eye. Because drilling a hole as far down as you'll have to is no piece of cake. One way to do the job is by using a good hand-turned bit brace. A bit brace and auger bit will make a clean hole, plus you'll have good control. It's going to be quite a challenge to your ingenuity if you use an auger bit with a standard length, because it will not penetrate all the way through the body. Usually a longer auger bit can be found at most nonfranchise, but well-equipped hardware stores. Look for a 12" to 15" long, 1" diameter auger bit. Some marine hardware stores also carry longer auger bits. A longer bit, aside from assuring you of the fact that it will go all the way through the body, will also keep your knuckles from scraping against the back of the mane as you grip and crank the turn handle. *(See Figure 152.)*

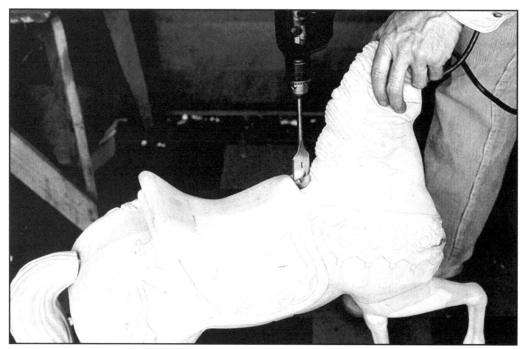

FIGURE 153 — *As an alternative, use a 1" diameter spade bit to start a hole in the body.*

The reason the auger bit has to be turned manually is because the end of the shank (called the tang, which is the part that fits into the drill chuck) will not fit into the chuck of a standard drill press or in that of a portable electric drill.

An alternative drilling method is to use a 1" diameter spade bit. Use a standard length to start the hole. *(See Figure 153.)* Drill down about two inches. Then, attach a drill bit extension. An extension will provide enough extra length so that you can drill through the body using a drill press or a portable electric drill. *(See Figure 154.)* Call around until you find a hardware store that sells extensions for

FIGURE 154 — *Attach a drill bit extension and complete the hole.*

spade bits. You can also find extensions available through tool supply catalogs.

When you've made a choice as to which tools you're going to use, decide exactly where you want to drill the hole. It can be drilled either forward of or right through the pommel. After you've decided, draw a vertical line straight down one side of the body and use it as a guide when you drill the hole. Stand back and make sure the line looks very straight to you. Hold a dowel, yard stick or some other rigid up-and-down object next to the pencil line to see if it is as straight as possible.

Next, make a punch mark with your awl at the point where the hole is to be drilled. It will help a great deal in assuring you of a more accurately drilled hole if you can get someone to assist in lining things up. It can be an awkward operation to pull off without a helping hand. And don't forget, the hole has to be drilled so that it's lined up straight not only from the side, but also when viewed from the front or the back.

If the hole gets somehow fouled up, an alternative solution is to cut a length of 1" diameter dowel to plug up the hole and shift gears regarding the insertion of a brass sleeve or other supporting pole. Simply attach the hooves to a wooden base so that the horse will be free-standing without a cylindrical support going through it. This method of securing the horse will be covered in the next section.

WOODEN BASE

If you're going to attach the horse to a wooden base, you'll need to decide on the particulars: size, shape, wood type, thickness, painted, stained, routed edges or plain. It's suggested that you not use a base that is more than $1\frac{1}{4}$" to $1\frac{1}{2}$" net thickness. Also, try to use a soft wood such as pine. The possibility always exists that as the horse is moved around from time to time, a heavy base could contribute to a crack in or a dislodgment of one or more of the legs. A lighter base would lessen your concern about damage should you have to transport the horse to, say— the Smithsonian or the lobby of the White House.

When the base is ready, place the horse on it and position it exactly where you want it to stand. (In case you haven't come to this conclusion yet, it's better to drill the holes into the base before you paint or stain it.) Then, draw an outline around each of the three hooves on the surface of the base. Remove the horse from the base.

The following operation is another one where a second pair of hands is very helpful. Insert a $^{13}\!/_{64}$" diameter twist bit into your portable electric drill. Place the wooden base on your work bench, close to one edge or near a corner. Put the horse on the base with the legs lined up over to one side of, but not on, the outlines of the hooves. The idea is for you to eyeball where the holes should be drilled up through the base at the correct angle in accordance with the angle of each leg. The $^{13}\!/_{64}$" bit should provide enough clearance for the shank of each screw. Before you begin drilling the holes in the base make sure the drill bit is parallel with the direction of each of the legs. Remember, this is only the base you're drilling into.

When the holes have been drilled through the base, double check the angle of each one. Insert a long nail, wire or drill bit into the holes, one at a time, and see if they line up with the angle of the legs. An additional step you can take at this stage is to countersink holes over the screw holes you just drilled in the base. These recessed wider holes will hide the heads of the screws, as well as keep the bottom of the base flush with whatever surface it will rest upon. If you do go ahead with countersinking holes use a $^{23}\!/_{64}$" counterbore, available at most hardware stores, or just use a $^{3}\!/_{8}$" wood bit to get the same basic result.

Back to the legs. Drilling holes up into the legs can be nerve-wracking when you realize you could possibly drill up into one or more of the legs and right on through the side of the wood. So be as careful as possible and take your time to avoid any unpleasant surprises. If an accident does happen, it's *merely a matter of patching up the hole* with wood filler or wood epoxy and following up with some sanding.

If you're ready to drill the holes into the legs, insert a $\frac{1}{8}$" diameter twist bit into your drill chuck. Next, place the hooves directly over the outlines on the base. The front leg seems to be the best choice to start with. Extend one end of the base, with the horse on it, over the edge of your work surface. Be sure the hoof covers the corresponding hoof outline you drew on the base. Now insert the drill bit up through the hole in the base, directly under the hoof, and begin drilling up into the leg. Before repeating this step on the other two legs, screw a 2", #10 flathead screw up into the front leg. This will help to hold the horse in place while you drill holes up into the other two legs. When the holes have been drilled into the remaining legs, secure them to the base the same way that you did the first leg.

SECURING THE BRASS SLEEVE

If you're going to use a brass sleeve there are two ways of making a solid connection to the base. One way is to place the horse, with the brass sleeve inserted through it, onto the base. Next, draw a circle around the bottom of the sleeve onto the base. Let the end of the brass sleeve touch the surface of the base. Remove the horse from the base. Drill a hole half-way into the thickness of the wood base, using a 1" spade bit. You might have to roll the bit around in the hole to enlarge it a fraction. See what the fit is like first. Place the horse back onto the base. About a half inch of the brass sleeve, at the bottom, should fit easily into the hole and provide an extra margin of stability for the horse as it rests on the base. *(See Figure 155.)*

FIGURE 155 *— Secure the brass sleeve to the base.*

FIGURE 156-1 — *Sand the horse and cover it with one application of sanding sealer and two applications of undercoating. Sand lightly between applications.*

FIGURE 156-2 — *Decide on a color scheme for your horse. A little creativity at this stage will go a long way towards a beautifully finished carousel horse.*

The other way to secure the brass sleeve to the base is with a 1" flange. File out the inner threaded area with a rat-tail file or a small half-round file. (Don't file off too much or you'll defeat the purpose of the flange, which is to secure the sleeve.) File the threads down a little bit, then check periodically to test the fit of the sleeve in the opening of the flange. When the sleeve fits tightly, draw a circle around the flange as it rests on the base. Make awl marks through the holes in the outer rim of the flange into the base. Remove the flange and drill small holes into the awl marks. Replace the flange and screw it down using $\frac{3}{4}$" screws. This arrangement will make a stable union of the horse, brass sleeve and base.

Figures 156-1 and 156-2 show the finished, but not painted, horse you've seen in gradually evolving stages throughout the workbook. At this stage, the horse has been covered with one application of sanding sealer and two applications of undercoating. The surface has been lightly sanded between applications. When you get to this point

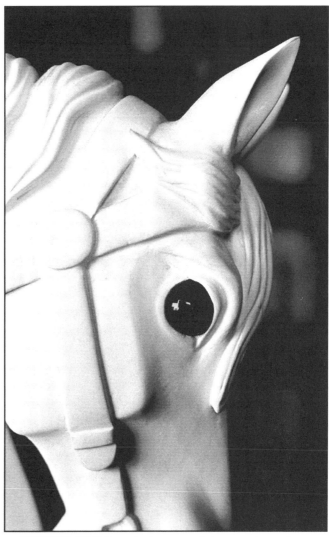

FIGURE 157-1 — A close-up of the eye shows how the face looks with the eye inserted and the area around the eye built up with wood epoxy.

you'll have before you the final challenge: what to do with the blank "canvas-in-the-round." Take your good old time deciding. If you put as much energy, thoughtfulness and creativity into your painting choices (whether you or someone else paints it) as you did in the carving, you'll end up with a magnificent carousel horse.

Figures 157-1 and 157-2 show close-ups of the face so you can more easily see the details. Additionally, you can see how the face looks with the eyes inserted. It makes a substantial difference in the expression; it makes the face come alive.

Figure 157-1 shows the notch cut in the corner of the eye as shown in Figure 129. Wood epoxy was used to build up the upper lid, and after it hardened, some of the surface on the inside of the lid was scraped off with a chip carving knife. When enough was scraped off, the eye was coaxed into place, but not too firmly until after the application of the paint.

FIGURE 157-2 — *Extra details are carved on the finished face. Add as many details as you feel comfortable carving.*

The full shot of the head is similar to Figure 137, except in this photograph the head is carved to completion. The relief carving of the small buckle and the tip of the strap, although a minor bit of carving, enhances the overall appearance of the face. It's one of those small touches that looks better included than left off. Relative to some headstraps this set is fairly basic. You could start out carving a basic design such as the one in the photograph. Then, if it seems too tame, you could drill holes in the center of the straps and insert small diameter glass jewels. Before you decide to go with jewels make sure you can live with all that glitter.

It may be of some interest to you to see how flowers were carved on each side of the horse, as examples of alternative carving techniques. The flowers on the left side of the horse were carved directly out of the wood on the horse: direct relief carving. *(See Figure 158.)*

On the right side, several generic flower heads were carved from wafer-thin pieces of wood. Cut-out, circular wood pieces were glued to a cardboard backing using rubber cement glue. After the flower heads were cared out, each one was carefully removed from the cardboard with a knife. Then small holes were drilled in the center of the back of each flower. Small diameter dowel pegs were glued to the back of the flower heads and plugged into holes drilled into the horse. *(See Figure 159.)*

These different approaches are to show you that if you should want to carve flowers, cherubs, angels, eagles or any other subjects that will project out from your horse, they can be carved either way.

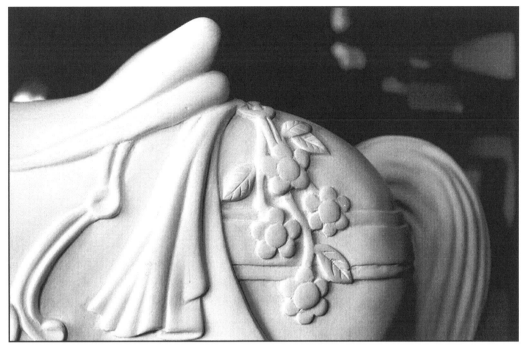

FIGURE 158 — *Details such as flowers and blankets can be carved directly into the wood of the horse so that they are raised up from the body in relief.*

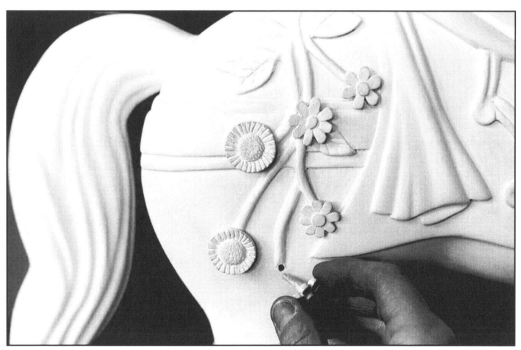

FIGURE 159 — *Alternately, details like these flower heads can be carved separately and glued to the horse.*

♞ *ABOUT THE AUTHOR* ♞

Ken Hughes taught carousel horse carving in Berkeley, California, using the $1/3$ size design for the horse blanks. In addition, he carved at a carousel restoration company in Oakland, Ca. on a freelance basis for several years. Currently, he does architectural illustration and is preparing a book on 19th century-style toymaking and one on historical architecture in San Francisco.